THE HA...
CROSSW...
COMPANION

compiled by
"SENIOR WRANGLER"
of THE LEADER

ODHAMS PRESS LIMITED
LONG ACRE - LONDON, W.C.2

First published 1932

Printed in Great Britain

FOREWORD

THIS HANDY CROSSWORD COMPANION has been specially prepared by "Senior Wrangler" of *The Leader*, and will be of inestimable value to all Crossword enthusiasts in their efforts to solve the many difficult problems which continually arise.

The great majority of alternatives already used in Crosswords are incorporated, set out in word size and in alphabetical order to facilitate easy reference.

Copious cross-reference has been made, so that, whichever likely word springs to the mind, it will in most cases be found in its proper place or easily traced. In some instances reference is definitely made in one set of solutions to a word in another. In any event, when you have discovered one likely solution, refer to the alternative given in its proper place to find other possibilities.

Even the many alternatives grouped together here will not of necessity answer your clue, as the clues themselves differ from time to time, so that it is essential that you consult your dictionary to ascertain whether any particular solution is applicable. Remember the clue is the key to the problem.

New alternatives will, of course, be continually cropping up and will have to be found as they arise.

When presented with a clue which indicates one of the particular sections of this book, a search through may reveal the solution required. In any event a glance at these will show how great are the possibilities for linking large numbers of them.

The interlocking group in Crosswords has been cleverly exploited by compilers. Sometimes words of seven or eight letters being linked up, with a few letters in either word the same. Usually, however, the trap is revealed by the appearance in the group of a fairly well-known solution. The use of the many sections of this volume may help you to discover the other links.

A good standard dictionary should be part of your library. Where a particular dictionary is specified by the compiler it is essential, of course, to have a copy of that volume.

Finally, when you have a clue calling for a solution in the plural it is advisable to turn also to the section wherein the singular form may be found and vice versa. The same applies equally to verbs in the past and present tense.

CONTENTS

THE HANDY
CROSSWORD COMPANION

2 Letters

Ab, Od
Ac, Bc
Ah, Eh, Oh, Ay
Ah, Lo, La
At, By, Up
At, On, To
Be, Am, Is
Bc, Ac
Bo, Ho, Lo, So, Wo, Yo
By, At, On
Cp, Cf
Di, Bi
Do, Go
Eg, Vg, Ex
Fy, Hi, Lo, La
Em, En
Ha, Hi, Ho
He, Me, We, Ye, My, Us
Hm, Sm
Io, Lo, Ho, Bo, Yo
La, Do, Fa, Re
La, Lo, Fy
Ma, Pa, Da
Ma, Ba, Am, Ab
Mi, Ti, Si
My, It
No, Na, Ne
Od, Os
On, In, Of, Up, To, At
Or, Au
Or, On
Pd, Pp, Pt
Pm, Am
Ra, Ri
Sm, Hm
Sa, Sd
St, Rd
We, Us
Ye, It
Yo, Bo, Lo, Io, Ho

3 Letters

Abc, Alp
Abe, Aby
Act, Ape
Act, Run
Ada, Ida
Add, Tot
Add, And, Aid
Ado, Ail
Aft, Oft, Eft
Age, Ago
Ale, Ama, Ava
All, Add
Ama, Ava
Ane, One
Any, Ary
Ape, Ass, Bat
Ape, Act
Apt, Fit
Arc, Art
Arm, Leg, Lap
Art, Ark
Ash, Asp
Axe, Awl
Aye, Yea, Yes
Baa, Bay, Yap

Bad, Sad, Mad
Bag, Box
Bag, Mag, Nap, Nab
Bag. Sac
Bag, Mat, Box
Bah, Pah, Poh, Yah
Bam, Fib, Lie
Ban, Bar
Bar, Law
Bat, Cat, Rat, Tat, Wat
Bay, Vae, Voe
Bay, Baa, Yap
Bed, Bud
Bed, Web
Ben, Den
Bet, Set
Bet, Bed
Bet, Peg
Bet, Bit
Bet, Web
Bey, Beg, Dey
Bib, Bub, Sip, Sup
Bid, Nod, Hie
Bin, Pig, Nog
Bit, Ort
Bit, But
Bit, Fig
Boa, Bom
Boa, Bow
Bob, Fob
Bob, Hog, Sol, Sou
Bob, Lob
Bob, Rob, Dob, Job
Bob, Dod
Bob, Bow
Bog, Sog
Bok, Elk, Yak
Boo, Coo, Moo
Bow, Bay
Bow, Cow
Box, Mix
Box, Bob
Box. Pyx, Pix, Bag, Bin
Boy, Son, Lad
Bud, Bur, But
Bug, Bee
Bum, Hum
Bur, Pur, Hum, Bum
Bur, Nur
But, Yet
But, Tub, Kid, Kit
But, Bar
Cab, Car
Cad, Pad, Cur
Can, Pan, Dan, Cat, Cap
Cap, Cop
Cap, Cup
Cap, Top
Cap, Hap, Nap, Lap
Car, Cab
Caw, Daw, Kaw
Cay, Key, Kay
Cob, Nob
Cod, Fob
Cod, Pod
Cod, Lob, Dab
Cog, Nog
Cog, Cot
Con, Den

Coo, Woo, Wow
Cor, Log, Ton, Tun
Cot, Won, Hut
Cot, Tot, Pot
Cow, Bow
Cow, Cob, Kob, Bok, Sow, Dog, Hog
Cub, Cur, Cob
Cup, Cub
Cup, Cap
Cup, Mug, Jug, Cap, Tug
Cut, Run
Cwt, Pwt, Dwt
Dab, Dad, Dub
Dab, Lob, Cod
Dab, Par, Hag, Bib
Dag, Dah, Jag
Dam, Dad
Dan, Can, Pan, Cat, Cap
Dan, Man
Dan, Ian, Jan
Daw, Caw, Kaw, Jay, Mag
Day, May, Ray
Den, Con
Den, Lie
Den, Pen, Ben, Pew
Dew, Wet, Ret
Dew, New
Dey, Bey, Beg
Dib, Rib
Die, Dim
Dig, Dip, Dug
Die, Dee
Dim, Die
Dip, Dop, Dap, Dib
Dip, Hip, Pip
Dip, Kip
Dob, Bob, Rob, Dod
Doe, Dog, Roe
Dog, Hug
Dog, Hog, Pig, Pug, Rug
Dog, Don
Don, Dom, Dan, Hon, Con
Dot, Jot, Tot, Lot, Mot
Dow, Hoy
Dun, Tan
Dub, Dab
Dun, Run
Dwt, Pwt, Cwt
Dye, Eye
Ear, Bar
Ecu, Sol, Sou
Ear, Lug (see Lip)
Eft, Aft, Oft
Eke, Ene, Ere
Eld, Old
Elf, Oaf, Elk
Elk, Bok, Yak
Elm, Yew
Ena, Ina, Una, Eve, Eva
Ere, Pre
Era, Age, Eon
Etc, Usw
Ewe, Doe
Eye, Dye
Eye, Eve
Fag, Lag

Fag, Gag
Fag, Sad
Fan, Nun
Fan, Van
Fat, Fit
Fay, Fey
Fee, Let
Fee, Feu, Due
Fen, Den, Pen
Fet, Hit
Fib, Lie, Lig, Bam
Fig, Fir
Fig, Bit
Fig, Rig
Fit, Apt
Fit, Hit, Sit
Fit, Fat
Fit, Fix, Pin, Tie
Fly, Sly
Fly, Ply
Fob, Bob
Fob, Fub
Fop, Sap, Oaf
For, Nor
Fox, Tod
Fox, Cod, Bob
Fum, Ruc
Gab, Gas
Gad, Bar
Gag, Tag
Gag, Fag
Gam, Sam
Gam, Jaw, Gab
Gap, Gat, Way
Gay, Day
Gay, Gey
Ged, Cod
Geo, Goe
Geo, Gio
Get, Net, Fet
Gig, Tig, Pig
Gin, Bib, Rum
Gin, Nix
Gin, Gen
Gin, Neb
Gin, Gun
Gin, Gig
Gob, Gam
Goe, Col
Got, Gat, Won
Gum, Sum
Gut, Gun
Gut, Run, Cut, Rut
Guy, Rum
Gyp, Gip
Had, Mad
Hag, Nag, Mag, Rag
Hag, Hog
Hag, Par, Bib, Dab
Hah, Pah, Bah, Yah
Ham, Jam, Yam
Hap, Lap, Wap
Has, His
Hat, Mat, Tat, Cap
Haw, Maw, Jaw, Paw
Hay, Haw, Hop
Hem, Rim
Hen, Pen, Pea, Kea
Hep, Hip, Pip
Hew, Mow
Hey, Hoy, Hem, Hep, Hup

Him, His
Hip, Pip
Hip, Hyp
Hit, Bit
Hit, Win
Hit, Tit
Hit, Rit
Hip, Lip, Lap
Hob, Hub
Hoe, Hob, Hod
Hog, Bob
Hog, Dog, Pig, Tag, Nag
Hog, Pug, Rug
Hop, Sow
Hop, Pop
How, Tor, Kop
Hoy, Hoa
Hoy, Dow
Hub, Nub
Hug, Dog
Hum, Bum
Hut, Cot, Won
Ian, Dan
Ice, Icy
Ida, Ina, Ada, Ira, Isa
Ilk, Irk
Inn, Ken
Ion, Ohm
Jab, Job, Jag
Jab, Dab
Jak, Oak, Sal
Jam, Ham, Yam
Jas, Jos, Job, Joe
Jaw, Gam, Gab
Jaw, Mag
Jaw, Rag
Jaw, Maw, Haw, Paw
Jem, Jim, Tim, Tom, Tam, Sam. Sim
Jet, Jut
Jig, Rig, Gig
Joe, Zoe
Jog, Dog
Jog, Rog
Jot, Bit, Tit
Joy, Joe
Jug, Jag
Jug, Mug, Tug
Jun, Jan
Jut, Put
Jut, Tut
Kaw, Caw
Kay, Key, Cay
Kea, Kae, Pea, Ket
Keg, Tig, Tug, Nog
Ken, Inn
Ken, See
Key, Kay, Cay
Kid, Kit, But
Kid, Kob, Kit
Kin, Kit
Kop, Tor
Lad, Cad, Tad, Pad
Lad, Son, Boy
Lag, Lug
Lag, Fag
Lag, Lax
Lag, Sag
Lam, Tan
Lap, Sip, Bib
Law, Lis
Law, Raj

Lay, Pay, Say, Way
Lay, Bet
Lea, Lee, Ley, Lay
Lea, Sea, Spa
Leg, Peg
Leg, Lap, Arm
Len, Leo, Lew
Let, Set, Net
Leu, Lev, Lew, Ley, Lei
Lib, Lab
Lid, Lip
Lie, Den
Lig, Lie
Lip, Lap, Ear, Hip
Lip, Tip, Rim
Lub, Cod, Dab
Lob, Log
Log, Jot
Log, Ton
Log, Leg
Log, Nog
Lop, Top
Lot, Cut
Lot, Pot, Dot
Low, Moo, Boo
Lug, Ear
Lug, Tug, Rug
Luz, Lug, Leg
Mad, Sad, Bad
Mad, Had
Mag, Peg, Meg
Mag, Bag
Man, Fan
Man, May
Man, Men
Mat, Oat
Mat, Pat, Wat
Mat, Tat, Hat
Mat, Lit
Maw, Jaw, Haw, Paw
May, Fay
May, Day
May, Mab
Met, Wed
Mew, Moa, Mag
Mew, Hen, Pen, Pea
Mix, Box
Mix, Mux
Mob, Mod, Mop
Moo, Coo, Boo
Mog, Wag
Mop, Moe, Mow
Mot, Dot
Mug, Jug, Tug, Cup
Mum, Rum, Bib, Rug, Bub
Nab, Nap, Bag
Nab, Rob
Nab, Nip
Nag, Hog
Nag, Mag, Rag, Hag
Nap, Nab, Bag
Nap, Nah, Nat, Neh
Nap, Nod
Nap, Nim, Nip
Nas, Nys, Nis
Nay, Not, Nor
Neb, Web
Ned, Ted, Neh, Nap
Neb, Gin
Nep, Net, Nef
New, Raw

Nib, Neb, Nub
Nib, Nog
Nib, Top
Nil, Nix
Nip, Sip, Dop
Nix, Pax, Poh, Bah, Pah
Nob, Nab
Nob, Fob
Nod, Bid
Nog, Cog
Nog, Pig, Bin
Nom, Tom
Nog, Keg
Nos, Num
Not, Nor, Non
Now, How
Noy, Nag
Nub, Nur
Nur, Bur
Nut, Fat
Nut, Nob
Oaf, Urf, Elf
Oaf, Sap
Oak, Jak, Sal, Bay
Oar, Tar, War, Jar
Oar, Bar, Tar
Oat, Mat
Oat, Cat, Bat
Oat, Awn, Bun, Ort
Obi, Oby, Aba
Oft, Aft, Eft
Ohm, Ion
Oil, Sil
Old, Eld, Odd
One, Ane
One, Odd
Orb, Arc
Ort, Bit
Out, But
Own, Owe
Pad, Paw, Pud
Pad, Cad
Pad, Wad
Pad, Paw, Pay, Pud
Pah, Bah, Pax, Nix, Poh
Pan, Can, Dan, Cat, Cap
Pan, Pin
Par, Dab, Hag, Bib, Ray
Par, Gar, Bar, Sar
Pat, Peg
Pat, Pet
Pat, Pam, Ray
Pat, Fit, Apt
Paw, Jaw, Haw, Maw
Pax, Nix
Pax, Pix
Pay, Put
Pay, Pat, Pal, Pax
Pea, Tea, Zea, Pia, Poa
Pea, Kea, Ket, Kac
Pea, Put
Peg, Bet
Peg, Meg, Mag
Peg, Teg
Peg, Leg
Pen, Pin
Pen, Pea, Hen, Kea
Pen, Pea, Mew, Hen
Pen, Mew, Pew
Pew, Bed
Pew, See, Set
Pie, Zuz

Pig, Tig, Gig
Pig, Pug, Pup
Pin, Rib
Pin, Tie, Fix
Pin, Nog, Peg
Pin, Win
Pip, Hip
Pix, Pax
Pix, Pyx
Ply, Fly
Pod, Cod
Pod, Pan, Pad
Poe, Pie
Poh, Foh
Poh, Pah, Yah, Bah
Pom, Pup, Pug
Pop, Pot
Pop, Dop
Pop, Hop
Pot, Fob
Pot, Set
Pot, Hob
Pot, Lot, Dot
Pot, Tot
Pot, Pop
Pre, Ere
Pry, Try
Pud, Tun, Ton, Tod
Pug, Pup, Pig, Rug, Tup
Pug, Tag
Pur, Bur, Hum, Bum
Put, Pot
Put, Rue
Put, Set
Put, Pit
Pwt, Dwt, Cwt
Pyx, Pix
Rad, Ran
Rag, Rig, Rug
Rag, Rat
Rag, Mag, Hag, Nag
Rag, Gag, Saw
Raj, Law
Ram, Jam
Ram, Rat, Pom, Tom
Ram, Dam
Ram, Tup, Teg, Hog, Tag
Ran, Run
Rap, Rip
Rap, Fan
Rap, Tap, Wap
Rat, Ram, Roe
Rat, Bat, Cat, Tat, Wat
Raw, New
Ray, Par
Red, Rud, Wan
Red, Sen, Yen
Ree, Rei, Red
Ret, Rot, Wet
Rew, Row
Rex, Roy, Roi
Rib, Pin
Rib, Dib, Luz
Rid, Red
Rig, Rag
Rig, Fig
Rig, Rim, Rib
Rim, Tip, Lip
Rim, Hem
Rob, Fob, Fub
Rob, Nab

Roc, Rok, Ruc
Roe, Doe, Dog
Rog, Jog
Rot, Rat
Row, Tow
Rub, Rud
Rug, Tug, Lug
Rue, Put
Rug, Pug, Pig, Hog
Rum, Mum, Rug, Bub
Run, Ran
Run, Cut, Gut, Rut
Run, Dun
Run, Ted
Run, Rum, Rub
Run, Act
Rye, Rie, Rue
Sac, Bag
Sac, Soc
Sad, Wan
Sai, Tat, Tag
Sal, Sol, Sam, Sim
Sal, Bay, Jak, Oak
Sam, Nap, Nat
Sam, Tam (*see* Jem)
Sap, Oaf
Saw, Sax, Dag, Zax
Saw, Gag, Rag
Saw, Say, Rag
Say, Bay
Say, Shy
Say, Way
Sea, Spa
See, Ken
See, Spy, Set, Eye
Seg, Teg, Tag
Seg, Set, Sow
Sen, Yen, Red
Set, Put
Set, Sat, Sit
Set, Bet
Set, Sex
Set, Pot, Seg
Set, Sow
Set, See
Sew, Hem
Sew, Wed
She, The, Who
She, His, Him
She, Sue
Shy, Coy
Sib, Syb
Sil, Oil
Sip, Nip, Bib, Bub
Sip, Nip, Sup, Lap
Six, Sax
Sky, Sly
Sob, Sos
Sog, Bog
Sol, Sou, Hog, Bob, Ecu
Son, Boy, Lad
Sow, Mow
S.R.S., F.R.S.
Tab, Tag
Tag, Dag
Tag, Tat, Sai
Tag, Teg, Pug, Rug, Seg
Tag, Dog
Tai, Tau
Taj, Top
Tam, Taj, Cap
Tan, Lam

Tan, Dun
Tan, Bay
Tap, Rap, Wap
Tap, Dap
Tap, Pat
Tap, Tag
Tap, Top, Tip
Tar, Tan, Tax
Tat, Wat, Bat, Rat, Cat
Tau, Tai
Taw, Tew
Taw, Tag
Taw, Rag
Taw, Tan
Tea, Pea, Zea
Ted, Run
Ted, Ned
Teg, Seg
Teg, Tag
Tew, Vex
The, Toe, Tie
The, Thy, She, Who
Tib, Tim
Tie, Tow
Tie, Pin, Fix
Tie, Two
Tig, Pig, Keg
Tig, Tag
Tim, Sim
Tin, Hin, Bin, Tig
Tin, Ton, Tun
Tin, Pin, Pen
Tip, Tig
Tod, Fox
Tom, Tam, Tim, Nom
Tom, Pom, Ram, Rat
Ton, Log
Ton, Tun, Tod, Pud
Top, Lop
Top, Cap
Top, Toy, Toe
Top, Cop, Tip, Tap, Tor
Tor, Kop, How
Tot, Put
Tot, Add
Try, Pry
Tub, But
Tub, Tun, Tig, Tot, Tug
Tut, Jut
Two, Twa, Ten
Una, Ina
Ure, Use
Ure, Elf, Oaf
Van, Fan
Van, Car, Cab
Van, Man
Vat, Fat, Vas, Cat
Vim, Vis
Voe, Vae, Bay
Wad, Pad
Wag, Mog
Wan, Sad
Wag, Wit
Wap, Hap
Wap, Rap, Tap
Wat, Wal, Wlr
Wat, Cat, Bat, Rat, Tat
Way, Gap, Gat
Way, Say, Lay, Pay
Web, Bet
Web, Neb
Wed, Wad

Wed, Sew
Wed, Met
Wet, Dew, Ret
Who, She, The, Thy
Win, Hit
Wit, Wot
Wit, Wag
Woe, Wae
Won, Hut, Cot
Won, Wan
Woo, Wow, Coo
Yah, Bah, Poh, Pab
Yak, Bok, Elk
Yam, Ham, Jam
Yap, Bay, Baa
Yea, Yes, Aye
Yen, Sen, Red
Yet, But
Yew, Elm
You, Thy
Zax, Sax, Saw, Dag
Zea, Pea, Tea
Zoe, Joe
Zuz, Pie

4 Letters

Abba, Abbe
Acid, Arid
Acop, Atop
Acts, Acta
Adam, Alan
Aery, Ayry, Airy, Eyry
Agee, Ajee
Ahas, Ahos
Aile, Apse
Airy, Spry
Akee, Aloe
Alex, Alec
Alme, Alma
Aloe, Sloe
Aloe, Akee
Also, Else
Amir, Emir
Anne, Anna
Anon, Enow, Soon
Anth, Anti
Apes, Aper
Arch, Arcs
Ares, Area
Arew, Arow
Arms, Army
Avow, Aver
Axes, Awls
Axis, Axle
Babe, Baby, Gaby
Back, Baft
Back, Cask
Baft, Haft
Bags, Pads, Bats
Bags, Rags, Fags
Bail, Pail
Bail, Writ
Bail, Ball
Bait, Brit
Bake, Fake, Cake
Bald, Bold
Bale, Bane
Bale, Lade
Ball, Bull
Ball, Gala
Balm, Palm, Calm

Balm, Palm, Holm
Balk, Bauk, Bilk
Band, Sand, Rand
Band, Gang
Band, Bend, Bind, Bond
Bane, Bale
Bang, Dong, Ding
Bank, Rand
Bank, Cant
Bank, Bink, Bunk
Barb, Pard, Mare, Hare, Hart
Barb, Bard, Bird
Barb, Dart
Bard, Lard, Nard
Bare, Bark, Pare
Bare, Lake
Bare, Bore
Bare, Rare
Bare, Bald
Bark, Back
Bark, Cork
Barn, Bawn, Byre
Bars, Bass
Base, Raca
Base, Bass
Bash, Dash, Lash, Wash, Pash
Bask, Mask
Bass, Bast
Bass, Dabs, Dace, Dare
Bast, Bark
Bath, Butt
Bath, Wash
Bats, Tits
Bawl, Yawl, Wawl, Waul
Beak, Peak
Beam, Leam
Beam, Bear
Beam, Team
Bean, Gean, Pear, Bear
Bear, Wear
Bear, Mean
Bear, Rear
Bear, Boar, Deer
Beat, Heat
Beat, Best
Beat, Belt, Welt
Beau, Bear, Beak
Beck, Beak
Beds, Bees
Bees, Bugs, Buns
Beet, Leek
Bell, Yell
Belt, Welt, Beat
Belt, Vest
Belt, Coat
Belt, Bolt
Bend, Tend, Wend
Bend, Bent
Bene, Bent, Beet
Bert, Bart
Bess, Tess, Jess
Best, Most
Bevy, Levy
Bide, Byde
Biff, Cuff
Biff, Buff, Puff, Huff
Bike, Bink, Hive
Bill, Will
Bind, Bine

Bind, Wind
Bins, Bing
Birr, Burr, Purr
Blad, Blot
Blay, Bley
Blot, Blur
Blot, Spot, Plot
Blot, Blet
Blot, Butt
Blow, Flow
Blow, Crow
Blur, Slur, Smut
Blur, Blot
Blue, Blae, Blee
Boar, Bear, Goat, Foal, Roan, Mohr
Boat, Flat
Boat, Butt
Bock, Hock, Sack
Body, Soul
Boer, Boor, Moor
Boll, Bolt
Boll, Noll, Poll
Boll, Ball, Bell
Bolt, Sort, Sift
Bolt, Bola
Bone, Bony
Bone, Hand
Booh, Pooh
Book, Hook
Book, Work, Tome
Boom, Loom, Toot
Boon, Good
Boor, Bear, Boob
Boot, Foot
Boot, Loot
Bore, Wore
Bore, Hole, Gore
Bore, Tire
Born, Bore
Bosh, Booh
Bosh, Tosh
Boss, Baas
Bout, Sour
Bowl, Boll
Bowl, Roll
Bowl, Cowl, Yawl
Brat, Wrap, Coat
Brew, Stew
Brim, Brow, Prow
Brit, Bret
Brit, Bait
Brow, Prow
Brow, Drum
Buck, Rack
Buck, Ruck
Buck, Musk
Buff. Cuff, Ruff
Bulk, Tome
Bump, Jump
Bump, Hump, Lump, Tump
Bund, Band
Bunk, Bunt
Bunt, Butt
Bunt, Punt
Burg, Bury
Burl, Burr
Burn, Bury
Burn, Hurt, Harm
Burt, Birt
Bury, Bush

Bush, Rush
Buss, Kiss
Bush, Bunk
Butt, Boat
Byre, Bawn
Caba, Cade
Cade, Tame
Cade, Jade
Cade, Calf
Cadi, Kadi
Cain, Kain
Cake, Bake
Calf, Colt, Wolf
Calf, Palm
Calk, Calx
Call, Sale
Call, Fall
Call, Carl, Paul
Call, Half
Call, Fare
Calm, Balm
Cane, Wand
Cane, Cask, Hand, Hank
Cane, Cany
Cant, Bank
Cant, Rant
Cant, Vent
Cape, Capa, Cope
Cape, Jupe
Cape, Naze
Caps, Cans, Cats
Card, Gift
Care, Cark
Care, Warn
Care, Cure
Carl, Myra, Mary, Mark
Carl, Paul, Call
Carp, Crab
Carp, Dart, Dare, Sapo, Salp
Cart, Carr, Care
Case, Vase, Cage, Cade
Case, Cask, Tank, Cast
Cask, Back
Cask, Hask, Tank
Cast, Emit
Cast, Shed
Cast, Last
Cast, Tint
Cath, Casy
Cave, Cove
Cave, Cafe
Cave, Ware
Cave, Cell
Cavy, Cony
Ceil, Veil
Cell, Well
Celt, Kelt
Cent, Mint
Cent, Dime
Cess, Sess
Chad, Shad
Cham, Khan, Shah
Cham, Imam, Shah
Chap, Chal, Chai
Chap, Clap
Chap, Chat
Char, Sear
Chat, Crax
Chay, Shay
Chew, Chaw
Chew, Chig, Diet

Chin, Shin, Skin
Chip, Chap, Clip, Snip, Chop
City, Site, Gite
Clam, Claw
Clam, Clog, Clag
Clan, Club, Crew
Clap, Slam, Slap, Flap
Claw, Craw, Crop
Clip, Grip
Clod, Clot, Clog
Clog, Shoe
Club, Drub
Clue, Clew
Coal, Coke, Peat
Coat, Boas, Hood, Coif
Coat, Wool
Coca, Kola
Cock, Duck, Rock, Rook
Cock, Nock
Cock, Rick
Coca, Coco
Coda, Mode, Code
Code, Tome, Coil
Cods, Pods
Cogs, Cods, Cops
Coif, Coil
Coin, Doit
Cola, Kola
Cold, Bold
Cole, Kale
Cole, Coln
Colt, Dolt
Colt, Belt, Welt
Comb, Kemb
Come, Came
Cony, Pony, Colt, Cavy.
Cook, Hoot
Cool, Poor
Cool, Cold
Coom, Culm
Coom, Soot, Sout
Coon, Coof
Coot, Cock
Cope, Cape, Capa
Cora, Dora, Nora
Corf, Corb
Cork, Bark
Corn, Horn, Wart
Corn, Core
Cost, Care
Cosy, Mask, Cask, Case
Cosy, Cozy
Cosy, Cosh
Cote, Cove
Cots, Cott
Crab, Clam, Cray
Cram, Flam
Crib, Drib, Prig
Crop, Craw, Claw
Crop, Chop, Chip
Crop, Reap
Crow, Blow
Crow, Brag
Cubs, Pugs, Pups, Rugs
Cuca, Ruta, Rusa
Cuff, Muff, Ruff
Cuff, Biff
Cuff, Puff, Buff, Fuff
Cull, Gull
Cull, Pull
Culm, Coom

Curb, Kerb
Cure, Pure
Cure, Care
Curl, Furl, Hurl
Curl, Tirl
Curr, Purr, Burr, Purl
Czar, Tsar, Ksar, Tzar
Dabs, Dace, Dare, Bass
Dace, Dart, Dare, Jack
Daff, Doff
Daff, Daft
Dale, Vale, Dell, Dean, Dene, Pale
Dali, Palm
Dame, Lady
Damn, Darn
Damp, Dank, Dark
Dang, Darn, Damn, Hang
Dare, Gage, Wage
Dare, Defy
Dart, Barb
Dark, Dirk, Dusk, Murk
Dash, Cast
Dash, Lash
Dash, Pash
Date, Rate
Daub, Gaum
Daud, Dawd
Daut, Dawt
Dave, Davy
Dawn, Morn
Daze, Maze, Faze
Dead, Read
Deaf, Dead
Deal, Teak, Dhak
Deal, Heap
Deal, Lead
Dean, Dell, Glen, Dene
Dear, Near
Deem, Heed
Deem, Ween, Reed
Deep, Keen
Deer, Bear, Dieb, Boar, Reem
Deft, Neat, Feat
Defy, Deny
Dell, Gill
Demi, Semi, Hemi
Dene, Dale, Vale
Dent, Dint, Dunt
Dent, Dene
Dhak, Teak
Dice, Dies
Dick, Jock, Jack
Diet, Chew, Chig
Diet, Meet, Leet
Dike, Dyke, Rine
Dike, Sike
Dime, Cent, Mite
Dims, Dips, Dies, Dibs
Dine, Diet, Dish
Ding, Ting
Dins, Duns
Dirk, Fork
Dirt, Mire
Dirt, Rust, Dust
Disc, Disk, Dish
Dish, Fish
Dish, Dash
Dock, Lock
Dodo, Dove

Does, Goes
Doff, Daff
Dogs, Dons
Doit, Coin
Dole, Dope, Dose, Doze
Doll, Dolt
Dole, Dule
Dolt, Colt
Dome, Home
Done, Gone
Dora, Cora, Nora
Dory, Dare
Dote, Love
Dour, Lour, Sour
Dove, Dodo, Sore
Down, Douf
Drab, Gray, Grey
Drag, Draw
Dram, Gram, Tron, Troy
Draw, Drew
Dray, Drag, Trap, Tram
Drib, Crib, Prig
Drib, Drip
Drip, Drop
Drop, Trap
Drow, Trow
Drub, Club
Drub, Drum
Drum, Brow
Duad, Dyad
Dual, Duel
Dubs, Dabs
Duce, Duke, Doge
Duck, Cock
Dude, Dupe
Duel, Duet
Duel, Dual
Dues, Fees, Feus
Dull, Mull
Dull, Pale
Dumb, Numb
Dumb, Mute
Dune, Dene, Drum
Dune, Runn
Dupe, Ruse
Dust, Cast, Last
Duty, Dues
Dyad, Duad
Dyes, Eyes, Hues
Earl, Jarl
Earl, Lars, Lord
Earn, Gain
Ears, Arms
Ease, Eath
Ease, Easy
East, West, Airt
Eats, Fats, Oats
Edge, Edgy
Edge, Urge
Edit, Emit
Edna (see Mona)
Ella, Elsa, Edna, Emma
Else, Also
Emir, Amir
Emit, Exit
Emit, Cast
Emma, Ella, Alma, Elsa
Enow, Soon, Anon
Epic, Epos
Esau, Evan
Evil, Vile, Vild
Ewes, Roes

Exit, Obit
Eyas, Nyas
Eyes, Dyes, Hues
Eyes, Eyne, Eine
Eyes, Eves
Faap, Carp
Face, Rage
Fade, Vade
Fake, Bake
Fail, Fall
Fair, Just
Fair, Maid
Fake, Take
Fake, Bake
Fall, Pall
Fall, Call
Fame, Name
Fame, Fauna
Fane, Vane
Fans, Raps
Fare, Farl
Fare, Care
Farm, Park, Mark
Farm, Ferm
Faro, Mora, Loto
Faro, Lark
Fast, Rash
Fate, Fame
Fawn, Faun
Faze, Daze, Maze
Feal, Leal, Real
Feat, Face
Feed, Heed
Feel, Feed
Feer, Fear, Frau
Feer, Fier
Fees, Feus, Dues
Fell, Film
Fell, Sell
Fell, Hill
Felt, Welt
Fend, Tend, Feed
Fent, Vent, Rent
Feod, Feud, Food
Fern, Herb
Fibs, Lies
File, Fife
Fill, Full
Fill, Hold
Film, Fell
Find, Fund
Fine, Nice
Fire, Pyre
Fire, Firk
Fire, Rile
Firm, Hard
Fish, Dish
Fits, Rigs
Flag, Flax
Flag, Flat
Flam, Cram
Flam, Sham, Hoax, Whim
Flap, Flip, Flop
Flat, Boat
Flat, Seat
Flay, Fley
Fled, Flew
Fled, Sped
Fled, Hied
Flee, Flow
Flip, Trip

Flip, Flap, Flop
Flit, Frit
Flog, Flat
Flog, Slog
Flop, Plop
Flow, Flux
Flow, Blow
Foal (see Boar)
Foam, Ream
Foes, Foen, Fone
Foil, Foin
Foil, Fail
Fold, Hold
Fond, Kind
Fond, Fand
Fone, Foen, Foes
Food, Fool
Food, Feod, Feud
Fool, Tool
Fool (see Loon)
Fool, Foil
Foot, Hoof
Foot, Boot, Coot, Root
Foot, Rood
Fork, Dirk
Form, Norm
Form, Sort
Form, Firm
Form, Turn
Fort, Port
Foul, Sour
Four, Hour
Fowl (see Fung)
Frap, Flap
Frap, Wrap
Frau, Frow
Frau, Feer, Fear
Fret, Fray, Frab
Fret, Swag
Fuff, Puff
Full, Fill
Full, Pull
Fund, Find
Fung, Runt, Ront, Fowl
Fury, Fume
Furl, Curl
Fuse, Fuze
Fuss, Rush
Gaby, Baby
Gael, Gaul
Gaff, Jeff
Gage, Dare
Gage, Wage, Game
Gage, Pale
Gain, Earn
Gain, Vail
Gain, Make
Gait, Walk
Gala, Ball
Gale, Harr
Gamb, Limb
Game, Gamy
Game, Jape
Game, Race
Gang, Ging, Ring, Pack, Band
Gaol, Jail
Gape, Gaze
Garb, Wont
Gash, Rase
Gasp, Pant
Gasp, Gaup, Gawp, Gape

Gate, Lane
Gate, Yate, Yett
Gaum, Daub
Gawd, Gaud
Gean, Bean, Pear
Gear, Wear
Geld, Pelf
Geld, Gold, Gilt, Gelt
Gibe, Jibe, Wipe
Gift, Give
Gift, Card
Gill, Mile
Gird, Garb
Girl, Gill, Jill
Girt, Gird
Gist, Gest
Gite, Site, City
Give, Gift
Glen (see Dale and Dean)
Glim, Slim
Glum, Grum, Grim
Gnar, Knar, Snar
Gnaw, Snap, Knab, Knap
Goad, Goal, Gold, Gowd
Goat, Boar, Foal
Goes, Gaes
Goes, Does
Golf, Goff, Gowf
Golf, Polo, Solo
Gone, Done
Gong, Sang
Good, Hoot, Toot
Good, Boon
Gore, Bore
Gout, Roup
Gowk, Gouk
Gowl, Yowl, Howl
Gown, Boun
Grab, Brag
Grab, Pram
Grab, Pull
Gram, Dram, Tron, Troy
Gray, Grey
Gray, Drab, Grey
Grin, Girn
Grip, Clip
Grip, Trip
Grip, Iron
Guan, Swan
Gule, Tule
Gull, Cull
Gull, Sell
Gush, Gust
Gust, Gout
Gust, Puff
Gwen, Owen
Haar, Harr, Hoar
Hack, Hash
Hack, Heck
Hack, Jack, Pick
Hack, Kick
Hadj, Hajj
Haft, Baft
Haft. Heft
Hail, Rain
Hail, Rail
Hail, Wail (see Wail)
Hair, Vair
Hair, Haik
Hake, Dace, Dart, Pike, Dare

Hake, Laze
Half, Call
Hale, Waly
Hall, Wall, Fall
Halm, Haum
Halt, Wait, Hold
Hand, Hank, Cane
Hand, Hind
Hard, Tart
Hard, Firm
Hare, Mare, Hart, Pard, Barb
Hang, Dang, Darn, Damn
Hark, Hail
Harm, Hurt, Tort
Harm, Maim
Harn, Lawn
Harp, Horn
Harr, Haar, Hoar
Harr, Gale
Hash, Mash
Hask, Cask
Haul, Harl
Have, Hath
Have, Save
Have, Take
Hawk, Lark
Haze, Maze, Faze, Daze
Head, Lead
Head, Peak
Head, Herd
Heap, Deal
Heap, Reap
Heat, Beat
Heed, Feed
Heed, Hear
Heed, Deem
Heel, Seel, Reel
Hell, Hele (see Peel)
Hell, Hole
Help, Yelp, Yell
Hemi, Demi, Semi
Hemp, Kemp
Hend, Hent
Herb, Fern
Herb, Hemp
Herd, Head
Herd, Host, Mort
Herd, Keep
Hern, Tern, Pern
Hero, Nero
Hers, Hern
Hest, Hist
Hide, Side
Hied, Fled
High, Rich
Hill, Fell
Hilt, Haft, Heft
Hind, Mink, Minx
Hint, Mint
Hish, Hist, Hush
Hiss, Pish
Hist, List
Hive, Live
Hive, Bike, Bink
Hive, Dive
Hoar, Haar, Harr
Hoax, Coax
Hoax, Sham, Flam
Hock, Sack
Hold, Holt, Hole

Hold, Fold
Hold, Hald
Hole, Mole
Hole, Sole
Hole, Hope, Howe
Hole, Bore, Gore
Hole, Bole
Holm, Palm, Balm
Holm, Cola
Home, Dome
Home, Hole
Home, Tomb
Home, Tame
Hone, Pine
Hoof, Foot
Hook, Nook
Hoop, Hoot
Hoop, Loop, Loup
Hoot, Cook
Hoot, Boom
Hoot, Honk
Hoot, Toot, Tout
Hope, Cove
Hope, Tope
Horn, Corn, Wart
Hors, More
Hose, Rose
Hour, Tour
Hour, Four
Howl, Gowl, Yowl
Howl, Bawl, Yawl
Huck, Jack
Huff, Fuff
Hues, Dyes, Eyes
Hugh, Hugo
Hulk, Husk
Hull, Hulk Helm
Hump, Bump, Tump,
    Lump
Hunk, Junk
Hunt, Punt
Hunt, Want
Hurl, Toss
Hurt, Harm, Burn
Hush, Tush, Hist
Hush, Mute
Idea, Idol
Idea, Whim
Idle, Idly
Idol, Icon, Ikon
Ilex, Ulex
Imam, Cham, Shah
Into, Unto, Onto
Into, Inly
Iota, Note
Irak, Iran, Iraq
Iris, Lois
Iris, Irid
Iron, Grip
Isle, Holm, Inch
Iwis, Ywis
Jack, Dace, Dare, Dart
Jack, Jock, Dick
Jack, Huck
Jack, Back, Sack
Jade, Cade
Jade, Jane, June
Jail, Gaol
Jake, Jane
Jann, Jinn
Jape, Game
Jape, Joke, Jest

Jarl, Earl
Jars, Wars, Mars
Jean, Joan
Jeff, Gaff
Jerk, Yerk
Jess, Bess, Tess
Jest, Josh
Jill, Gill, Girl
Jibe, Gibe, Wipe
Joke, Jape
Jole, Joll
Jole, Jowl
Jole, Vola, Nose
Jove, Love
Jouk, Jook
Jump, Romp, Ramp
June, July
Junk, Tank, Cask, Husk
Junk, Punt
Junk, Hunk
Junk, Meat, Meal
Jupe, Cape
Just, Fair
Just, Jest
Just, List
Kadi, Cadi
Kagu, Kaka
Kail, Kale, Kali, Gale
Kain, Cain
Kale, Cole
Kama, Cama, Kami
Keek, Peek, Seek
Keek, Peer, Peep
Keen, Deep
Keep, Kept
Keep, Neep
Keep, Heed
Keep, Herd
Kelt, Celt
Kemb, Comb
Kemp, Hemp
Kerb, Curb
Kern, Kirn
Kick, Lick, Tick
Kids, Kine
Kilp, Kelp
Kind, Mild
Kind, Mode
Kind, Tint
Kind, Fond
Kind, Sort
Kink, Link, Wind
Kipe, Kist
Kipe, Pipe
Kiss, Buss
Kite, Kyte
Kite, Tike
Kite, Kiwi
Knap, Knot, Knop,
    Knar, Knag, Knob,
    Knur
Knar, Snar, Gnar
Knit, Knot
Knob, Knub, Knur,
    Knop
Know, Trow
Kola, Cola
Kola, Coca
Koba, Zobo
Ksar, Tsar, Tzar, Csar
Kurd, Turk
Lack, Lass

Lade, Last
Lady, Dame
Laid, Lain
Lake, Tone, Saxe
Lake, Mere
Lamb, Lama, Barb
Lame, Game, Limp,
    Gamy
Lame, Tame
Lane, Line
Lane, Gate
Land, Sand, Rand
Lard, Nard, Bard
Lark, Hawk
Lark, Faro
Lash, Gash, Dash
Lass, Lady
Lass, Pass
Last, Late
Last, Past
Last, Cast
Last, Dust
Late, Last
Lava, Moya
Laze, Hake
Lazy, Lusk
Lead, Head
Lead, Bear
Lead, Deal
Lead, Load
Lead, Tend
Lead, Leam
Leal, Feal, Real
Leam, Beam
Lean, Weak, Mean
Leap, Skip, Lope
Leap, Loup
Leat, Leet
Leek, Weed, Beet
Left, Went, Late
Legs, Lens
Lena, Zena
Lend, Loan
Lent, Lend, Send,
    Sent
Less, Loss, Lass, Lose
Levy, Bevy
Lice, Mice, Tick
Lies, Fibs
Life, Wife
Lift, Life
Lift, Loft
Lill, Gill, Jill
Lill, Loll
Lily, Lucy
Limb, Gamb
Lime, Pome, Pine
Limp, Lisp
Limp, Lame, Game
Limp, Jump, Leap
Line, Lane
Line, Wire
Ling, Vine
Link, Ring, Rink
Link, Lunt
Link, Line
Lint, Line
Lint, Tent
Lion, Lynx
Lira, Lire, Para
List, Hist
List, Just

List, Lest
List, Leet
List, Lust
List, Tilt
Lith, Limp
Live, Vive
Liza, Lisa
Load, Pood
Loan, Lend
Lobs, Logs
Lock, Cork
Lock, Cock
Lock, Dock
Loft, Lift
Lois, Iris
Lone, Lane
Lone, Sole, Sola, Soli, Sole
Long, Lang
Long, Want
Long, Lone
Loof, Poop
Look, Loom, Seem
Loom, Boom, Toot
Loom, Loof
Loon, Coon, Fool, Coof
Loon, Coot
Loon, Loom
Loop, Loup, Hoop
Loos, Mons, Lens
Loot, Boot
Lord, Look
Lord, Lars, Earl
Lord, Peer
Lore, Lare
Lose, Rase
Lose, Loss
Loss, Lass
Loto, Ludo
Loto, Faro
Loto, Golf, Gowf
Loup, Leap
Lour, Dour, Sour
Love, Dove
Love, Jove
Love, Like
Love, Move
Love, None
Love, Dote
Ludo (see Loto)
Lugs, Tugs, Ties, Rugs
Luke, Lucy
Lump, Dump
Lunt, Link
Lure, Term
Lure, Toll, Tole
Lusk, Lazy
Lust, List
Lute, Lure, Lyre
Lynx, Manx
Lynx, Lion
Mace, Vare
Mage, Magi
Maid, Maud
Maim, Maul
Maim, Harm
Main, Pair
Main, Rain
Make, Gain
Make, Sake
Make, Mate
Make, Form

Make, Made
Make, Take
Make, Sake
Maki (see Saki)
Mall, Maul
Mall, Walk
Malm, Maum
Malm, Maul, Maim
Many, Nine
Mare, Barb, Pard, Hare, Hart
Mark, Park
Mark, Merk
Marm, Maam
Mars, Moon
Mary, Myra, Vera
Mash, Hash
Mash, Mush
Mash, Mast
Mask, Bask
Mass, Tass
Mast, Pole, Post, Pale, Pile
Mast, Mail
Mate, Fate, Make
Maul, Mall
Mazy, Hazy
Meal, Meat, Veal, Lean
Mean, Meek
Mean, Near
Mean, Lean
Mean, Bear
Mean, Moan
Meat, Junk
Meat, Seat
Meat, Meal, Veal, Lean
Meek, Mean, Mild
Meet, Moot
Meet, Leet, Diet
Meet, Mate
Melt, Bolt, Pelt
Mend, Wend
Mere, Bare, Pure
Mere, Pale
Mere, Lake
Mess, Mass, Muss
Mess, Toss
Mess, Soss
Mess, Mesh
Mete, Rate
Mete, Mile
Mete, Mere, Meer
Mien, View
Miff, Tiff
Mild, Meek
Mild, Kind
Mild, Wild
Mile, Gill
Mile, Mete
Mile, Pole
Milk, Silk
Mill, Mull
Mill, Pull
Mina, Myna
Mine, Line
Mink, Minx, Mina, Lynx
Mint, Mite, Cent
Mint, Cent
Mint, Vint
Mint, Hint, Wink
Mire, Mere
Mire, Dirt

Miss, Lass, Loss
Miss, Pass
Mite, Dime
Mite, Mote
Mite, Bite
Moan, Roar
Moan, Roin
Mode, Code, Coda
Mode, Make
Mode, Wont
Mohr, Mole, Moco, Mule, Moke, Mare, Sore, Vole, Tabr, Thar
Moil, Toil
Mole, Hole
Mole, Pile
Mole, Mote
Mome, Moke, Mope
Mona, Edna, Dora, Nora, Cora
Mood, Mode
Moon, Coon
Moon, Mars
Moon, Noon, Morn, Dawn
Moor, Boor, Boer
Moot, Meet
Mope, Dote
More, Hors
Mort, Host, Herd
Mote, Mite, Moth
Mote, Mole
Mora, Faro
Moss, Soss
Most, Best
Move, Rove
Move, Love
Muck, Ruck
Muff, Buff, Ruff, Cuff
Muff, Mule
Mule, Rule, Pole
Mule, Mole, Male
Mull, Dull
Mull, Mill
Murk (see Dark)
Mush, Pass, Move
Musk, Buck
Mute, Lute
Mute, Hush
Mute, Dumb
Myra, Mary
Nail, Tail, Hair, Vair
Nail, Tack
Name, Dame, Nome, Fame
Name, Fame, Fama
Nard, Lard, Bard
Naze, Cape
Neap, Deep
Neal, Neil
Neap, Repp
Near, Dear
Neat, Newt
Neat, Nett
Neat, Feat, Deft
Neat, Nout, Nowt
Neil, Neol
Nest, Rest
Nice, Fine
Nick, Nock
Nick, Pick, Tick
Nigh, With

Nine, Many
Noah, Noel
Nock, Cock
Noes, Nays
Noll, Poll, Boll
None, Love
None, Nine, Five
Nook, Hook
Nora, Dora, Cora
Norm, Form
Nose, Vola, Jole
Nose, Rose
Note, Tone
Note, Iota
Null, Nude, Rude
Numb, Dumb
Nyas, Eyas
Obit, Exit
Udal, Udal, Alod
Odes, Poems
Oily, Wily
Olla, Olio
Ondy, Wavy
Onyx, Opal
Orgy, Orge
Ours, Ourn
Ouse, Oise
Over, Upon
Over, Oner
Owen, Gwen
Oyes, Oyez, Oyer
Paca, Pala, Paco
Pace, Race, Rack
Pack, Sack
Pack, Back, Hack, Sack
Pack, Gang, Ging, Ring
Page, Pane
Pail, Sail, Saic, Bail
Pair, Main
Pair, Twin
Pale, Vale
Pale, Gage
Pale, Pile, Pole
Pale, Paly, Dull
Palm, Calf
Palm, Dali, Dhak
Palm, Balm, Holm
Paly, Waxy
Pant, Gasp
Pant, Want
Papa, Pope
Para, Lira
Pard, Barb
Pare, Bare
Park, Mark, Farm, Yard
Parr, Carp
Part, Page
Pash, Gash, Bash, Wash,
  Lash, Dash
Pass, Path
Pass, Move, Mush
Pass, Lass, Loss
Pass, Miss
Past, Post
Pate, Tete
Paul, Pawl
Paul, Saul
Paul, Carl, Call
Peak, Beak
Peak, Head
Pear, Teak
Pear, Gean

Peat, Coal, Fuel
Peba, Zebu, Zobo
Peck, Pick
Pech, Pegh
Peat, Peer, Lord
Peel, Pell, Pill, Pelt, Fell,
  Hell, Hele
Peep, Peer, Peek, Leer,
  Keek, Perk
Peep, Weep
Peer, Pear, Lord
Pelf, Geld
Pell, Fell, Veil
Pelt, Polt
Perk (see Peep)
Pern, Hern, Tern
Pert, Perk
Pets, Vets, Bets
Phew, Whew
Pice, Pies
Pick, Pink
Pick, Pack
Pick, Hack, Jack
Pied, Eyed
Pike, Pink, Pope
Pile, Pyre
Pile, Pole, Pale
Pine, Hone
Pine, Vine, Tine, Lime
Ping (see Ring)
Pink, Wink
Pink, Punt
Pink, Pike, Pope
Pink, Tint, Tone
Pint, Gill
Pint, Link, Line
Pipe, Pupe
Pipe, Tile
Pipe, Kipe
Pips, Pops
Pish, Hiss
Plat, Plan, Plot
Play, Ploy
Play, Pray
Plop, Flop
Plop, Plap
Plot, Shot, Plat
Plug, Shag
Pods, Cods
Poem, Poet
Poem, Odes
Poke, Cope, Robe, Hose,
  Mode, Toge
Pole, Mile
Polk, Polo
Pole (see Mast)
Polo, Solo, Loto, Ludo
Polo, Golf
Poll, Boll, Noll
Pome, Pine, Lime
Pond, Pool
Pood, Load
Pood, Rood
Pooh, Booh
Poon, Toon
Poop, Loof
Poop, Port
Poop, Prow
Poor, Cool
Pope, Pike
Pope, Tope, Sole
Pope, Papa

Pore, Port
Pore, Bore, Gore, Hole,
  Bole
Port, Fort
Port, Wort
Port, Pork
Post, Pose
Post, Mast
Pout, Tout
Pout, Moue
Pram, Grab
Pram, Tram, Trap, Dray
Prig, Drib, Crib
Prog, Brog, Prod
Prow, Brow
Prog, Pray
Prop, Stop
Pudu, Puma
Puff, Gust
Puff, Huff, Fuff
Pugs, Rugs, Cubs, Pups
Puke, Puce
Pule, Tube
Pull, Bull
Pull, Full
Pull, Cull
Pull, Mill
Puma, Zuna
Punt, Bunt, Kent
Punt, Pink, Junk
Puny, Tiny
Pure, Mere, Bare
Pure, Cure
Purl, Pull
Purl, Curl
Purr, Purl, Curr, Burr
Push, Rush, Gush
Pyre, Pile
Pyre, Fire
Quab, Quob
Quad, Quod
Quad, Quay
Quib, Quip, Quiz
Quid, Shad, Scad
Raca, Base
Race, Pace, Rate
Race, Rise, Rash
Race, Game
Race, Rase, Raze
Race, Pace, Rack
Race, Ride
Rach, Rack
Rack, Sack
Rack, Rick
Rack, Buck
Rack, Walk
Raft, Waft
Rage, Rile
Rage, Face
Rail, Rain, Hail
Rail, Sail, Mail
Rain, Hail
Raja, Rana, Rani
Raki, Sake
Ramp, Romp, Jump
Rand, Bank
Rang, Rung, Rong
Rang, Sang
Rank, Rasp
Rank, Bank
Rant, Cant
Rare, Rara

Rare, Bare
Rare, Tang
Rase, Lose
Rase, Rake
Rase, Race, Raze
Rase, Gash
Rash, Rush
Rash, Fast
Rasp, Risp
Rate, Tare
Rate, Fare
Rate, Rule
Rate, Mete
Rate, Race
Rate, Date
Rats, Yaks
Rave, Rage, Rate
Read, Redd
Read, Dead
Real, Leal, Feal
Ream, Foam
Ream, Seam
Reap, Heap
Reap, Crop
Rear, Read
Rear, Bear
Reed, Weed, Seed
Reed, Ween, Deem
Reef, Reel, Veer
Reek, Reel
Reel, Seel, Heel
Reem, Deer
Rees, Reis, Real
Reis, Reds, Raps
Rend, Rent, Tear
Rent, Fent, Vent
Rent, Lend
Rent, Rend
Repp, Neap
Rest, Nest, Tent
Rest, Sist
Rest, Rely
Rest, Beat
Rhea, Shea
Rial, Ryal, Real
Rich, Rife
Rich, Much, High
Ride, Rule
Ride, Rode, Rade
Ride, Side
Rife, Tide
Rift, Riot
Rigs, Fits
Rigs, Rags, Togs
Rile, Fire
Rile, Rage
Rima, Riva
Rime, Rive
Rime, Lime
Rind, Rine
Rine, Dike
Rine, Rone, Rune
Ring, Ging, Gang, Pack
Ring, Rink
Ring, Ting, Ding, Sing, Ping, Tang
Riot, Rile
Risp, Rasp
Risp, Rise
Rive, Riva
Roan, Foal
Roan, Rose

Roar, Soar
Roar, Moan
Robe, Cope, Copa
Rock, Rook
Rock, Rota
Roes, Ewes
Roin, Moan
Roll, Poll
Roll, Bowl
Romp, Ramp, Jump
Rood, Foot
Rood, Pood
Roof, Hood
Roof, Rone
Roof, Room
Rook, Cook
Rook, Rock, Cock, Duck
Rook, Coot
Rook, Fool
Room, Roam
Room, Roum
Roop, Roar
Root, Foot, Sole
Root, Rout
Rope, Tape
Rosa, Rose
Rose, Nose
Rose, Posy
Rose, Rone
Ross, Soss
Rote, Koto
Roup, Gout
Rout, Root
Rout, Tout
Rove, Rave, Rake
Rove, Move
Ruby, Ruth
Ruby, Guly
Ruby, Rosy
Ruby, Ruff
Ruck, Duck, Ruff
Ruck, Muck
Ruck, Tuck
Ruck, Buck
Rudd, Ruff
Rude, Nude, Null
Ruff, Runt
Ruff, Cuff, Buff
Rule, Mule, Pole
Rung, Sung, Rang, Sang
Runn, Dune
Runs, Cuts
Rusa, Musk, Tutu, Ruta, Rush, Ruse
Ruse, Dupe
Rush, Fuss
Rush, Fast
Rush, Bush
Rust, Dust
Ruta, Rusa, Cuca (see Rusa)
Ruts, Cuts, Guts
Ruts, Runs
Sack, Hock
Sack, Pack
Safe, Some, Sure
Safe, Save
Sage, Sago, Sego
Sage, Sane, Safe
Saic, Sail, Pail, Bail
Sail, Slip
Sail, Saic, Pai

Sake, Make
Sake, Raki
Saki, Vari, Maki, Zati
Sale, Call
Sane, Tang
Sane, Safe
Sang, Rang
Sang, Sung
Sang, Gong
Sank, Sunk
Sapo, Salp, Carp
Sark, Sari, Sack
Saul, Paul
Save, Have
Saxe, Lake
Scab, Swab
Scab, Scar, Star, Sear
Scad, Shad
Scar, Sway
Scat, Seat
Scot, Shot
Scow, Snow, Dhow
Scud, Spud
Scum, Scun, Scud
Scun, Scon
Seal, Seam, Seat
Seal, Near
Seal, Seat
Seal, Seel
Seal, Teal
Seam, Ream
Seam, Drum
Sear, Char
Sear, Scar
Seat, Flat
Sect, Sept
Seel, Heel, Reel
Seel, Pell
Seel, Seal
Seem, Peer, Peep, Peek, Keek, Perk
Seem, Look
Seep, Weep
Seep, Sipe
Sell, Gull
Sell, Seel
Sell, Seat
Sell, Tell
Semi, Demi, Hemi
Sent, Vent
Sent (see Lent)
Serb, Serf, Sorb
Serg, Serj
Sess, Cess
Shad, Chad, Quid
Shag, Swan
Shag, Plug
Shah, Khan, Cham
Sham, Hoax, Flam, Whim
Shay, Chay
Shea, Rhea
Shed, Cast
Shin, Skin, Chin
Ship, Skip, Saic
Shoe, Clog
Shot, Plot, Plat
Shot, Spot
Shot, Stot
Show, Stow
Show, Shew
Show, Spot

Show, Sham
Sice, Syce
Sick, Sunk
Side, Ride
Side, Wide
Side, Hide
Sift, Sile, Silt
Sift, Sort, Bolt
Sike, Syke
Sike, Dike
Silt, Salt
Silt, Sipe
Sind, Synd
Sine, Syne
Sing, Song
Sing, Ring
Sipe, Silt, Seep
Sire, Sirs
Sist, Rest
Site, City, Gite
Sith, With
Sits, Sets
Size, Line
Skim, Swim, Skin, Veil
Skin, Shin, Chin
Skin, Veil
Skio, Skeo
Skip, Slip
Skip, Leap, Lope
Skip, Skim, Skin
Skip, Skep
Skit, Twit
Skit, Skip
Skug, Scug
Slab, Slat
Slab, Slob
Slam, Snap
Slap, Clap, Slat, Slay
Slat, Blad
Slay, Slew
Slim, Glim
Slim, Thin, Lean
Slip, Snip
Slip, Sail
Slip, Trip
Slit, Slot
Slob, Slub
Sloe, Slae, Aloe
Slog, Flog, Slap
Slue, Slub
Slug, Thug
Slug, Slut
Slur, Blur
Smew, Smee
Smit, Smut
Snag, Snig
Snag, Snar
Snap, Slam
Snap, Knap
Snap, Knap, Gnaw
Snar, Gnar, Knar
Sneb, Snib, Snub
Snig, Snip, Snap
Snob, Snod
Snob, Snot
Snub, Slur
Snug, Smug
Soap, Soup
Sobs, Woes
Soft, Mild
Soho, Toho, Yoho
Soil, Moil

Soil, Mool
Soil, Foul
Sold, Told
Sole, Lone
Sole, Welt
Solo, Sola, Sole
Song, Solo
Song, Sing
Soon, Anon, Enow
Soot, Sout, Coom
Soot, Spot
Sore, Dodo, Dove
Sore, Vari, Moke
Sort, Soft, Mild
Sort, Form
Sort, Mode
Sort, Bolt, Sift
Sort, Kind
Soss, Mess
Soss, Ross
Soul, Saul, Core
Sour, Lour, Dour
Sour, Tart
Sour, Spur, Scur
Sour, Foul
Span, Spun
Spar, Swap, Slap
Sped, Fled
Sped, Hied
Spit, Spet
Spit, Spat, Spot
Spot, Shot
Spot, Show
Spot, Blot, Plot
Spud, Scud
Stay, Stem, Stop, Staw, Whoa
Stay, Seat
Step, Stop
Stew, Brew
Stir, Star, Spur
Stir, Stot
Stop, Prop
Stop, Stow
Stot, Stag
Stow, Show
Stub, Stud
Stub, Stob
Such, Sich
Suck, Tuck
Suet, Salt
Suit, Writ
Suke, Suky, Susy
Sure, Safe
Sure, Some
Swad, Swab
Swag, Fret
Swam, Swum
Swan, Guan
Swat, Slat, Spat
Sway, Stay
Sway, Trap
Swop, Swap, Chop
Tack, Nail
Tack, Race
Tack, Tuck
Tahr, Mohr, Thar
Take, Have
Take, Tony
Talc, Gold
Talk, Tale
Tame, Lame

Tame, Home
Tame, Cade
Tang, Sane
Tang, Rare
Tank, Cask (see Junk)
Tape, Rope
Tape, Type
Tape, Tapa
Tare, Rate
Tare, Tara, Taro
Tart, Hard
Tash, Tass
Tass, Mass
Teak, Pear
Teak, Deal, Dhak
Teak, Teil
Teal, Seal
Team, Beam
Tear, Tirr
Tear, Rend
Tear, Wear
Tede, Tead
Tell, Yell, Sell, Bell
Tend, Mind, Heed
Tend, Lead
Tend, Bend, Wend
Tent, Lint
Term, Lure
Tern, Teal
Tern, Pern, Hern
Tess, Jess, Bess
Test, Pest
Test, Tent, Tout
Tete, Pate
Than, That
Thar, Tahr, Mohr
That, What
Them, Thee, They, Thou
Then, When
Thin, Glim, Glib
Thin, Lean, Slim
Thug, Slug
Tick, Lick, Firk, Birk
Tick, Tuck
Tick, Lice, Mice
Tide, Time
Tide, Rife
Tier, Tiff
Ties, Tugs
Tiff, Tift
Tiff, Miff
Tift, Rift, Riot
Tike, Tyke
Tile, Tire
Tile, Tilt
Tile, Tube
Tile, Pipe
Tile, Pule
Till, Tile
Tilt, List
Tilt, Tent
Tilt, Tile
Time, Name
Tind, Tine
Tine, Pine, Ling, Vine, Pink
Ting, Ring, Ping, Ding
Tint, Tone, Pink
Tint, Cast
Tiny, Puny
Tire, Bore
Tire, Tyre

Tirl, Turn, Curl
Tiro, Tyro
Tits, Bats
Toco, Toko
Toga, Toge, Togs
Toge, Cope (see Poke)
Togs, Rags, Rigs
Toil, Moil
Toil, Work, Book
Told, Teld
Told, Sold
Tole, Toll, Lure
Tomb, Home
Tome, Code
Tome, Book, Work
Tome, Tone
Tome, Bulk
Tone, Tune
Tone, Mode
Tone, Tint, Blue
Tony, Taky
Tool, Viol
Tool, Fool
Toom, Void
Toon, Poon
Toot, Loom, Boom
Toot, Tout
Tope, Pope, Sole
Tore, Torn, Worn, Wore
Tort, Harm, Hurt
Tosh, Bosh, Tush, Pish
Toss, Hurl
Toss, Mess, Mush
Tots, Sots
Tots, Adds
Tout, Pout, Moue
Tout, Lout
Tout, Hoot, Toot
Tows, Taps
Trap, Sway
Trap, Drop
Trap, Tram, Dray, Pram, Drag
Trey, Tray
Trey, Trio
Trim, Trig, Prim
Trim, Clip, Slip
Trip, Flip
Trip, Slip
Trip, Trap
Trip, Trot
Tron, Troy
Trow, Drow
Trow, Know
Tsar, Czar, Tzar, Ksar
Tube, Tyre
Tube, Pule
Tube, Tuba
Tuck, Tack
Tuck, Tick
Tuck, Ruck
Tule, Gule
Tune, Rune
Tump, Bump, Lump
Turn, Warp
Turk, Kurd
Tush, Tusk
Tush, Hush, Hist
Tuck, Suck
Twin, Pair
Twit, Skit
Udal, Odal, Alod

Ulex, Ilex
Unto, Into, Onto
Upon, Over
Urge, Edge
Utas, Utis
Vade, Fade
Vail, Veil
Vail, Gain
Vain, Void
Vair, Hair
Vale, Dale (see Dale)
Vale, Pale
Vane, Fane
Vara, Hand, Yard, Acre
Vare, Mace
Vare, Cane
Vari (see Saki)
Vase, Case
Veer, Wear
Veil, Ceil
Veil, Vest
Vent, Cant
Vent, Fent, Rent
Vera, Mary, Myra
Vest, Belt
Vice, Vise
View, Mien
Vile, Vild, Evil
Vile, Vice
Vine, Tine, Pine, Lime
Vine, Ling
Vine, Pink
Vine, Wine
Vint, Mint
Visa, Vise
Viva, Vive
Vive, Live
Vola, Jole, Nose
Volt, Jolt, Bolt
Vole, Mole (see Mohr)
Waft, Raft
Waff, Yaff
Wage, Gage, Game
Wage, Dare
Wail, Hail, Waul, Wawl, Call
Wait, Halt
Walk, Mall
Walk, Gait
Walk, Rack
Wall, Hall, Fall
Wall, Well
Waly, Hale
Wand, Cane
Want, Pant
Want, Long
Ward, Warp
Ward, Ware, Warn
Ware, Wore
Ware, Cave
Warn, Care
Warm, Hard
Warp, Turn
Warp, Cast
Warp, Wash
Warp, Ward
Wars, Jars, Mars
Wart, Corn, Horn
Wary, Ware
Wash, Bath
Wave, Wawe, Wake
Wavy, Ondy

Wawl, Yowl, Yawl, Gowl
Waxy, Paly
Weak, Meek
Weak, Lean, Mean
Weak, Weal
Wear, Bear
Wear, Gear
Wear, Veer
Wear, Weir
Weed, Seed, Reed
Weed, Leek, Beet
Week, Year
Ween, Deem, Reed
Weep, Peep
Weep, Seep
Weir, Wear
Weld, Weed
Well, Dell, Cell
Well, Weal, Weel
Welt, Belt, Pelt, Beat, Best
Welt, Felt
Welt, Sole
Welt, Whip
Wend, Wind, Wynd
Went, Left
Wept, Weep
Were, Wert
West, Lead
West, East, Airt
What, That
When, Then
Whew, Phew
Whim, Idea
Whim, Whip
Whim, Flam
Whip, Whop, Whap
Whip, Writ
Whip, Whig
Whip, Whiz, Whid
Whir, Whur
Wide, Side
Whiz, Whir
Wild, Mild
Will, Bill
Will, Wilt
Will, Wish, Wull
Wily, Oily
Wind, Wynd, Wend
Wine, Vine
Wink, Pink
Wipe, Gibe, Jibe
Wire, Wiry
Wise, Ware, Wary
With, Nigh
With, Sith
Woes, Sobs
Woes, Waes
Wolf, Colt, Calf
Wold, Wood
Wont, Garb
Wood, Food
Wool, Woom, Coat
Wore, Bore
Wore, Ware
Work, Book, Word
Work, Wark
Wort, Port
Worn, Wore, Torn, Tore
Wrap, Frap
Wrap, Trap
Wrap, Brat, Coat

Writ, Bail
Writ, Suit
Yaff, Waff
Yaks, Rats
Yard, Vara, Hand, Acre
Yawl, Yowl, Hail, Howl
Yead, Yede
Yean, Yeen
Year, Week
Yede, Yead
Yell, Yelp
Yell, Bell
Yelp, Peep
Yerk, Jerk
Yett, Yate, Gate
Yoho, Soho, Toho
Yolk, Yelk
Yowl, Yawl, Gowl
Ywis, Iwis
Zany, Gaby
Zati (see Saki)
Zarf, Zurf
Zena, Lena
Zest, Gust
Zion, Sion
Zobo, Zebu, Peba
Zoll, Poll, Toll

5 Letters

Aback, Abaft
Aback, Aloft
Abase, Abash, Abate, Abuse
Abbes, Abbas
Abide, Abode
Above, About
Abysm, Abyss, Chasm
Adopt, Adapt, Shape
Aerie, Ayrie
Afrit, Scrat
After, Later
Agile, Swift
Agley, Aglee
Agree, Apply
Aided, Bided, Sided
Alant, Eland
Alarm, Scare
Alden, Olden
Alder, Elder
Alick, Aleck
Allow, Allot
Algum, Almug
Alive, Agile, Alert
Along, Among
Amber, Umber
Ambit, Orbit
Amend, Emend
Amine, Amide
Amity, Unity
Among, Emong
Among, Along
Ample, Large
Ankle, Ancle
Apeak, Apeek
Apert, Overt
Apple, Maple
Apply, Agree
Apron, Acton
Aptly, Fitly
Archy, Archd
Arias, Dries

Ashen, Ashes
Ashen, Aspen
Aught, Ought
Avail, Avale
Avert, Evert
Avoid, Evade
Aware, Awake
Azure, Azury, Azurn
Baccy, Bacco
Badge, Ridge
Baize, Beige
Baize, Gauze
Bajan, Bejan
Baked, Baken
Baked, Faked
Baler, Bales
Balls, Rails, Dowls
Balls, Bolls, Bulbs
Balmy, Barmy
Banco, Bench
Banks, Links
Bared, Naked
Basil, Basel
Basis, Bases, Basal
Bawls, Yawls, Yowls
Beano, Feast
Bedad, Begad
Beech, Larch, Birch
Began, Begun
Begat, Begot
Begum, Negus
Beige, Baize
Belle, Bella
Berry, Merry
Berth, Birth
Berob, Strip
Besom, Broom
Beset, Besit, Befit
Betty, Jemmy, Jenny
Betty, Bessy, Betsy
Bevel, Bezel
Bevel, Gayel
Bevel, Level, Lever
Bided, Sided, Aided
Bidet, Civet, Zibet
Bilge, Bulge
Birch, Larch, Beech
Bison, Vison, Urson
Bitch, Fitch
Black, Flush
Black, Bleak
Black, Blank
Bland, Blank
Bland, Plain
Blank, Frank
Blank, Black
Blare, Blast
Blare, Blore
Blast, Boost, Boast
Blaze, Flame, Flare
Bleak, Blank, Black
Bleak, Bream
Blirt, Flirt
Blobs, Blows, Blots
Blood, Brood
Bloom, Shock
Bloom, Blood
Blown, Flown
Bluff, Cliff
Blunt, Bluff
Blush, Flush
Board, Boord

Boast, Boost
Bodle, Noble, Ruble
Bogey, Bogie
Boggy, Soggy, Moory
Boiar, Boyar
Bolas, Bolus, Bolts
Boles, Boxes
Booby, Looby, Loony
Boots, Coats, Shoes
Booze, Boose, Bowse, Bouse
Boson, Bosun
Bound, Fount
Bourn, Bound
Brace, Trace
Brace, Grain
Brack, Break
Brack, Crack
Braid, Plait
Brail, Trail
Brain, Brawn
Bravo, Brave, Brava
Brawl, Growl
Brawl, Broil
Break, Wreck
Bream, Bleak
Breed, Speed
Brief, Crisp
Brier, Briar
Brill, Prill, Troll
Brine, Briny
Brock, Crock, Crook
Brool, Crool
Broth, Brose
Broth, Froth
Brush, Brash
Brute, Bruin
Budge, Nudge
Build, Built, Erect
Build, Breed
Bulge, Surge
Bulse, Burse, Purse
Bumbo, Jumbo
Bumps (see Humps)
Bunco, Bunko
Burly, Bulky, Bully
Burro, Zorra, Zorro
Burst, Brust
Burst, Split
Bushy, Busky, Bosky
Caaba, Kaaba
Cabas, Cades, Cages
Cabob, Nabob
Cabot, Sabot
Caged, Cased, Caved
Cages, Cases, Cades
Calif, Kalif
Calix, Calyx, Palea
Calls, Cauls
Camel, Capul
Canal, Canoe
Candy, Kandy
Caneh, Kaneh
Caple, Sable
Carve, Slice
Carve, Curve
Carry, Ferry
Casks, Masks
Catch, Latch
Cates, Cakes, Dates, Pates
Cause, Raise

Cease, Death
Cease, Close, Cesse
Cease, Peace
Cease, Leave, Cesse
Cents, Penny, Pence
Chack, Snack
Chaco, Shako
Chain, Braid
Chalk, Shale
Chaps, Chops
Chare, Chore
Chars, Shark, Charr
Chase, Chace
Chase, Frame
Chasm, Abysm, Abyss
Chick, Chuck
Chick, Child
Chime, Chimb
Chine, Spine, Spina
Chirk, Chirl, Chirm, Chirp, Chirr
Chirp, Cheep
Chirr, Churr
Chivy, Chevy
Chops, Swops
Chuck, Cluck, Clock
Chuff, Chump
Chump, Chunk
Churl, Chuff, Chump
Cider, Cyder
Cimar, Simar, Cymar
Cinch, Pinch
Cissy, Sissy, Missy
Civet, Genet, Bidet, Zibet
Civic, Civil
Clack, Click, Clock, Cluck
Clamp, Cramp, Clasp, Grasp
Clang, Clank
Claws, Flews
Clear, Sheer
Cliff, Clift, Bluff
Cliff, Cloff, Cleft
Clink, Clunk, Clank
Cloke, Cloak
Close, Dense
Cloth, Crash
Cloud, Crowd
Clour, Clout
Clump, Plump
Coach, Teach
Coats, Pants, Boots
Cobra, Copra
Cocos, Cocas
Cogie, Cogue
Colin, Robin
Comus, Momus
Cooee, Cooey
Corno, Cornu
Corny, Horny
Corse, Torso, Torse
Cough, Sough
Count, Compt
Cover, Covey
Coyly, Shyly
Crack, Brack
Crack, Craze
Crane, Crake, Drake
Crape, Orale
Crash, Quash, Crush, Smash, Frush

Crash, Crape
Crash, Clash
Crass, Gross
Crawl, Drawl, Prowl
Craze, Crack
Craze, Crase
Creak, Croak
Crepe, Crape
Cress, Grass
Crimp, Crisp
Crisp, Brief
Crock, Dirty
Crock, Crook
Crock, Brock
Croma, Crome
Cromb, Crome
Crook, Crank
Crool, Brool
Crool, Croon
Croon, Crool
Croon, Groan
Crowd, Drove
Crowd, Group
Cruet, Crust, Crout
Crush, Frush
Crush, Press
Cumin, Lupin
Cured, Fumed
Cured, Pured
Curve, Tarve
Cushy, Mushy, Gushy
Cutty, Patty
Daisy, Pansy, Tansy
Dally, Delay, Tarry
Dance, Wince
Darky, Dusky
Dates (see Cates)
Daunt, Haunt
Death, Cease
Deave, Deeve
Defer, Refer, Deter
Delay, Tarry, Dally
Demit, Remit
Demon, Leman, Devil
Demon, Felon
Denis, Denys
Dense, Close
Dense, Terse
Dense, Dunce
Deter, Refer, Defer
Deter, Debar
Devil, Demon, Leman
Devil, Satan
Dhole, Whale
Dicks, Dikes
Dicky, Micky
Dicky, Dirty
Digit, Eight
Dilly, Dilli
Dingy, Pinky
Dingy, Dirty
Dirty, Crock
Divan, Sedan
Diver, Liver
Diver, Dives
Dodge, Hedge
Dolce, Douce
Dolly, Polly, Molly
Doric, Ionic
Dorse, Doree
Dotty, Potty
Doura, Durra

Douse, Dowse, Souse
Drain, Train
Drake, Crake, Crane
Drank, Drunk
Drawl, Crawl
Drave, Drove
Drear, Dread
Dress, Drest
Dries, Arias
Drill, Twill
Drily, Dryly
Drink, Empty
Drink, Skink
Drink, Drank, Drunk
Drook, Drouk, Drown
Dross, Dregs, Gross
Drupe, Prune, Grape
Dryad, Oread
Dummy, Mummy
Dumps, Mumps
Dunch, Punch
Dusky, Murky
Dusty, Dirty
Dusty, Fusty, Rusty, Musty
Dwalm, Dwaum
Eager, Eagre
Eager, Edged
Earth, Garth
Egged, Urged, Edged
Eider, Wader, Jager
Eight, Digit
Eirie, Eerie
Eject, Evict
Eland, Alant
Elate, Exalt
Elder, Alder
Elder, Older
Eloge, Elogy
Elogy, Eloge
Elope, Elude, Slope
Elude, Evite, Evade
Elvan, Elfin
Embar, Embay
Embed, Imbed
Emend, Amend
Emmew, Immew
Emong, Among
Empty, Drink
Enact, Exact
Endow, Endue, Endew
Endow, Allow, Allot
Endue, Indue
Ennui, Annoy
Enrol, Enter
Ensue, Issue, Ensew
Enure, Inure
Envoi, Envoy
Erect, Build, Built
Erect, Exalt
Erode, Erase
Essay, Assay
Evade, Avoid
Evade, Elude, Evite
Evert, Avert
Evict, Eject
Exact, Evict
Exalt, Elate
Fable, False
Faint, Faded
Fairy, Faery
Faked, Baked

Fancy, Guess
Fanny, Nanny, Nancy
Fares, Wares
Fatal, Natal, Feral, Final, Fated
Feast, Beano
Feeze, Teaze
Feint, Faint
Fells, Dells
Felon, Demon
Fends, Tends
Fenks, Finks
Ferly, Early
Ferry, Carry
Fetch, Retch, Reach
Fetid, Tepid
Fifty, Fifth, Sixth, Ninth, Sixty, Forty
Filch, Pinch
Fines, Lines
Fiord, Fjord
Fired, Aired
First, Worst
Firth, Frith
Fitch, Bitch
Fitly, Aptly
Fitte, Fytte
Flame, Phare
Flare, Flame, Blaze, Glare
Flash, Plash
Fleck, Speck
Fleer, Sneer
Fleet, Sleek
Flews, Claws
Flier, Flyer, Fleer
Flies, Flees
Flies, Plies
Flies, Flits, Flips
Fling, Sling
Flirt, Blirt
Flite, Flyte
Flout, Scout
Flown, Blown
Flung, Slung
Flush, Blush
Flush, Black
Foggy, Muggy
Foods, Goods
Force, Farce
Fossa, Fosse
Fouat, Fowat
Fouls, Soils
Found, Fling, Flung
Fount, Bound
Foule, Toile
Fouth, Fowth
Fowls, Foals
Frack, Freck
Frame, Chase
Frame, Drape
Frame, Grain
Frame, Raise
Frank, Brisk
Frank, Brant, Crane
Frank, Blank
Fraud, Frost
Friar, Frier, Prior
Frisk, Brisk
Frisk, Flisk
Frock, Smock, Stock
Frock, Trick

Froze, Frore
Frump, Tramp
Frush, Crush
Fubby, Fubsy, Tubby
Fuggy, Muggy
Fumed, Cured
Funds, Purse
Funny, Sunny
Furze, Gorse
Fusee, Fuzee, Fuses
Fusty, Dusty, Musty, Rusty
Gaily, Gayly
Games, Gages, Wages
Garth, Earth
Gaucy, Gawcy, Gawsy
Gaudy, Showy
Gauze, Baize
Gauge, Gouge
Gavel, Bevel
Gemmy, Jemmy
Genet, Bidet, Civet, Zibet
Getup, Setup
Ghost, Ghoul
Giber, Jiber
Gigot, Jigot
Giles, Miles, Moses
Gipsy, Gypsy
Girds, Gives
Giron, Gyron
Girth, Width
Gives, Gyves
Glade, Slade
Glade, Place
Glare, Stare
Glare, Flare
Glass, Flask
Glazy, Glary
Glide, Slide
Gliff, Glift
Glist, Glisk
Globe, Glebe
Gloss, Gloze
Gnarl, Knarl, Snarl, Knurr, Knurl
Gnarr, Snarl, Gnarl
Goods, Foods
Gorse, Furze
Gourd, Mould
Graft, Graff
Grail, Graal
Grain, Brown
Grain, Braid
Grape, Drupe, Prune
Grasp, Clamp, Clasp, Cramp
Grass, Cress
Grate, Graze
Grave, Heavy
Grave, Grace
Great, Grand, Giant
Grece, Grese, Grees
Greit, Greet
Greta, Freda
Grice, Grise
Gride, Gryde, Grate, Grind
Grill, Broil
Grime, Grimy
Groan, Croon
Grope, Probe

Grope, Grape
Grosh, Groot, Groat
Gross, Crass
Group, Troop
Growl, Frown
Growl, Brawl
Growl, Prowl, Proll
Guess, Fancy
Gulch, Gully
Gurly, Burly, Surly
Gusty, Gushy
Gusty, Testy
Gutta, Gutty
Hadji, Hajji
Hairy, Vairy
Hallo, Hello, Hillo, Hollo, Hullo, Holla
Halve, Carve
Handy, Happy
Happy, Merry
Hards, Hurds
Harsh, Stern
Hasty, Haste
Hatch, Patch
Haunt, Daunt
Heals, Helps
Heals, Seals, Seams
Heavy, Heady
Hedge, Dodge
Heavy, Grave
Heavy, Weary
Hello (see Hallo)
Henna, Senna
Henry, Henri
Heron, Serin
Hetty, Betty, Netty
Hewer, Sewer
Hight, Hecht
Hilda, Tilda
Hills, Fells
Hills, Wilds
Hoise, Hoist
Holes, Holds, Holts
Hollo, Holla (see Hallo)
Honey, Money
Horns, Hoofs
Horny, Corny
Horse, Hound, Mount
Horse, Morse
Hovel, Hotel
Hovel, Haven
Howff, Houff
Hullo (see Hallo)
Hully, Husky
Human, Heman
Humps, Bumps, Mumps, Lumps, Tumps
Humpy, Tumpy, Lumpy
Hunch, Bunch
Hurds, Hards
Hurra, Huzza
Hurry, Haste
Hurry, Harry, Herry
Hythe, Hithe
Ideas, Idols
Idols, Idola, Icons, Ikons
Idols, Ideas
Idyll, Idyls
Ileum, Ilium
Ileac, Iliac
Imago, Image
Imbed, Embed

Imbar, Embar
Immew, Emmew
Indue, Endue
Inept, Inapt, Inert, Unapt
Inlet, Inset
Inset, Immit
Ionic, Doric
Irate, Wrath
Isles, Islet
Issue, Ensue, Ensew
Istle, Ixtle
Ivied, Ivyed
Jabot, Sabot, Rabat
Jacks, Packs, Decks
Jager, Wader, Eider
Jager, Yager
Jehad, Jihad
Jemmy, Betty, Jenny
Jetty, Jutty
Jiber, Giber
Jigot, Gigot
Joint, Joist
Joker, Poker
Joust, Giust
Jumbo, Bumbo
Junta, Junto
Kaaba, Caaba
Kaiak, Kayak, Umiak
Kalif, Calif
Kaneh, Caneh
Kedge, Kidge, Kedgy
Khaki, Shade
Kiley, Kyley
Kithe, Kythe
Knarl (see Gnarl)
Knars, Knags, Snaps
Knead, Mould
Knell, Knoll
Knosp, Kiosk
Koban, Toman
Koran, Quran
Krang, Kreng
Krans, Kranz
Label, Lapel
Label, Libel
Laden, Laded
Lagan, Ligan
Lager, Latex, Water
Lance (see Poise)
Lanes, Lakes
Lanky, Lathy
Larch, Beech, Birch
Large, Ample
Latch, Catch
Later, After
Latin, Ladin
Laver, Liver
Laver, Liner
Leach, Leech
Leafy, Leavy
Lease, Leave
Leash, Lease
Leave, Yield
Leave, Cease, Cesse
Ledge, Ridge
Ledum, Sedum
Leets, Meets
Leman, Demon
Lemon, Limes
Lemon, Melon
Level, Lever, Bevel

Levin, Leven
Liana, Liane
Light, Sight
Light, Night
Light, Wight
Limes, Lemon
Linen, Linin
Liner, Laver
Lines, Fines
Links, Banks
Lines, Pipes
Lions, Swine
Lists, Links
Liter, Litre
Litre, Livre, Metre
Lithe, Lythe, Withy
Liver, Diver
Livid, Lurid, Nitid
Llano, Llama
Loach, Roach
Looby, Booby
Loofa, Luffa
Loose, Vague
Lorry, Larry, Lurry
Loser, Loses
Louse, Mouse
Loved, Lover
Lover, Wooer
Lucid, Lurid
Lunch, Munch
Lupin, Cumin
Lurry, Hurry
Lusty, Vasty
Lutes, Lures
Lyart, Liart, Liard
Mabel, Hazel
Madam, Mamma, Mammy
Madge, Rudge, Radge, Rodge
Manes, Hades
Mania, Panic
Maple, Apple
Maray, Moray, Muray, Murry
March, Month
Marge, Verge
Marge, Madge, Marie
Masks, Casks
Mater, Pater
Matty, Patty
Maund, Pound
Mebos, Melon
Medal, Metal
Meets, Leets
Melic, Music
Melon, Lemon, Mebos
Merry, Happy
Merry, Berry
Metif, Metis
Metre, Meter
Metre, Litre
Micky, Dicky
Milly, Billy, Dolly, Polly, Molly
Misdo, Misgo
Missy, Cissy, Sissy
Mitre, Tiara
Molar, Malar
Molly, Polly, Dolly
Money, Penny
Momus, Comus

Mooch, Mouch
Moody, Moony, Morne
Moory, Boggy, Soggy
Moose, Mouse
Mopsy, Popsy, Topsy
Morne, Moody, Moony
Morne, Mound, Mount
Moses, Miles, Giles
Motor, Rotor, Robot
Mould, Gourd
Mould, Found
Mould, World
Mould, Knead
Mould, Round
Mound, Mount, Morne
Mount, Hound
Mouse, Moose, Morse, Horse
Mouse, Louse
Muddy, Mussy
Muffs, Mufti, Cuffs, Ruffs
Muggy, Foggy
Muley, Mooly
Mulsh, Mulch
Mummy, Dummy
Murky, Dusky
Mushy, Cushy
Music, Melic
Mussy, Messy
Musty, Fusty
Musty, Fuggy, Muggy
Myope, Myops
Nabob, Nawab, Sahib
Naked, Bared
Named, Nempt
Nanny, Nancy, Fanny
Nasty, Tasty
Nasty, Catty
Nebel, Rebec
Neddy, Teddy
Neddy, Noddy, Cuddy
Needy, Weedy, Seedy
Neeld, Neele
Negus, Begum
Neigh, Heigh
Nelly, Sally, Belle
Nerve, Verve
Netty, Hetty, Betty
Night, Light
Nitid, Vivid
Nixie, Pixie
Noble, Bodle, Ruble
Noisy, Rousy
Nonet, Nonny
North, South, Rhomb
Notch, Natch
Nudge, Budge
Nymph, Sylph
Oasis, Oases
Ochre, Ocher
Odeon, Odeum
Olden, Alden
Older, Elder
Olive, Alice, Clive, Elise
Oorie, Ourie
Opine, Think
Orale, Crape
Orate, Prate
Orbit, Ambit
Oread, Dryad
Ottar, Attar
Ought, Aught

Ousel, Ouzel
Outdo, Outgo
Overt, Apert
Oxlip, Tulip
Palay, Papaw
Palea, Calyx
Panda, Pong
Panic, Mania
Pansy, Daisy, Tansy
Pants, Coats
Pappy, Sappy, Nappy
Pardi, Pardy
Pasha, Pacha
Pasty, Patty
Patch, Hatch
Patch, Pitch
Pater, Mater
Pates, Cates
Patin, Paten
Patty, Cutty
Paven, Pavin, Pavan
Pavid, Timid
Payee, Payer
Peace, Cease
Peach, Pears
Peach, Teach
Pears, Peers
Pease, Pulse, Mulse
Pebas, Pumas
Penny, Money
Penny, Pence, Cents
Perch, Tench
Perch, Loach, Roach
Perch, Bench
Perse, Serge
Petal, Sepal
Petty, Petit
Petty, Potty
Pewit, Pewet, Pipit
Phare, Flare, Flame
Piano, Plane
Picul, Pecul
Piece, Patch
Piece, Slice
Pigmy, Pygmy
Piker, Hiker
Pinch, Punch, Dunch
Pinch, Cinch
Pinch, Filch
Pines, Pomes
Pinky, Dingy
Pipal, Pipul
Pipes, Lines
Pitch, Perch, Torch
Pitch, Patch
Pixie, Nixie
Plain, Bland
Place, Space
Plain, Clear
Plain, Frank
Plait, Pleat
Plait, Plaid
Plait, Braid
Plane, Plate
Plash, Flash
Plash, Plesh
Pleat, Plait
Plier, Plyer
Plies, Plods
Plies, Flies
Pluck, Plume
Pluck, Shuck

Plump, Clump
Plump, Slump
Plums, Prune
Poems, Poesy, Poets
Poise, Peise, Paise, Payse, Lance
Polka, Volta
Polts, Putts
Poser, Poses
Potty, Dotty
Pound, Poise
Pound, Maund
Pound, Round, Sound
Prank, Prink
Prank, Knack
Prate, Orate
Prawn, Brawn
Press, Brush
Press, Crush
Press, Dress, Prest, Drest
Press, Wrest
Price, Pride, Prize
Pride, Grade
Prier, Pryer
Prime, Primo, Prima
Print, Point
Prior, Friar, Frier
Prise, Prize
Prize, Pryse
Prize, Prime, Price
Proll, Prowl
Proof, Prief
Prose, Prosy
Proud, Stout
Prove, Probe, Grope
Prowl, Crawl, Proll
Prune, Plums, Pears
Prune, Grape, Drupe
Pucka, Pukka
Pudgy, Podgy, Pudsy, Pursy
Pumas, Pebas, Pacas
Punch, Hutch
Punch, Dunch
Purse, Burse, Bulse
Pursy, Puffy
Quake, Shake
Quart, Quire
Quash, Smash (see Crash)
Quass, Kvass
Queen, Quean
Quell, Quail
Quick, Quirk
Quick, Swift, Fleet, Agile
Quilt, Twilt
Quipu, Quipo
Quook, Shook
Quran, Koran
Rabat, Sabot, Jabot
Racer, Pacer
Racks, Rocks, Locks
Raise, Frame
Raise, Cause
Ramee, Ramie
Rands, Ranks, Rants
Rased, Raked
Rates, Rules
Rates, Raves, Rages
Rates, Taxes
Ravin, Raven
Razed, Razee

Ready, Handy
Realm, Reame
Reast, Reest, Reist
Reata, Riata
Reave, Reive
Rebec, Nebel
Rebel, Refel, Repel
Reddy, Ruddy
Reefs, Reels
Refel, Repel
Refer, Defer
Regal, Royal
Reins, Veins
Relay, Repay
Remit, Demit
Resin, Rosin, Roset
Rests, Beats
Retch, Reach
Rhine, Rhone, Rhune
Rhyme, Rhime
Rides, Tides
Ridge, Badge
Ridge, Ledge
Rived, Riven
Roach, Loach, Perch
Roast, Toast, Reast
Robin, Colin
Robot, Rotor, Motor
Rodge (see Madge)
Rohan, Rowan
Roric, Rural
Rough, Tough
Rough, Ruggy
Round, Mould
Round, Rough
Round, Pound, Sound
Rouse, Roust
Rousy, Noisy
Route, Round
Routh, Fouth
Rover, Roger, Rider
Rover, Cover
Rowdy, Dowdy, Rough
Rowed, Towed
Ruble, Noble, Bodle
Rubus, Rubia
Rudge, Rodge, Radge, Madge
Rugby, Rummy
Rules, Ruler, Miles, Poles
Rukhs, Runts, Ruffs
Rural, Roric
Sable, Caple
Sabot, Sayon
Sabot, Jabot, Rabat
Sacre, Saker
Sahib, Nabob, Nawab
Sails, Ships, Saics
Sally, Nelly, Belle
Salop, Salep
Salpa, Talpa
Salue, Salve
Saner, Safer
Saner, Sager, Wiser
Sappy, Pappy
Sappy, Soppy
Satan, Devil
Sauce, Spice
Sauch, Saugh
Sault, Vault
Sault, Swift, Fleet
Scale, Shale

Scale, Scalp
Scald, Scold, Scaud
Scald, Small
Scamp, Knave, Tramp
Scare, Spare
Scare, Alarm
Scarf, Scart, Skart
Scarf, Scarp
Scelp, Skelp
Scene, Scena
Scons, Scuns
Scoop, Sloop, Stoop
Score, Short
Scorn, Scoff, Spurn
Scoup, Scour
Scout, Flout
Scran, Skran
Scrap, Scran
Scrat, Afrit
Scrod, Shred
Scrub, Shrub
Scudi, Scudo
Sculk, Skulk
Scurf, Scuff
Sects, Sorts
Sedan, Divan
Sedum, Ledum
Seedy, Needy, Weedy
Seems, Seeks
Seize, Sease
Seize, Reive
Sends, Hurls
Senna, Henna
Sense, Sence
Sepal, Petal
Serfs, Serbs
Serge, Cerge
Serge, Perse
Serin, Heron
Setup, Getup
Sever, Split
Sewer, Hewer
Sewin, Sewen
Shack, Scale
Shack, Tramp
Shade, Flame, Sable
Shade, Shady, Swale
Shady, Shaky
Shaft, Shank
Shake, Quake
Shako, Chaco
Shale, Scale
Shall, Shalt
Shalm, Shawm
Shape, Adopt, Adapt
Shape, Phase, Shade
Shape, Think
Shard, Sherd, Shred
Share, Shave
Shark, Sharp
Shark, Charr, Chars
Sharp, Smart
Shave, Suave
Sheal, Sheil
Sheer, Clear
Shell, Sheal, Shale
Shift, Fleet
Shine, Shiny
Shine, Smile
Shire, Third
Shirk, Slink
Shirt, Skirt, Shift

Shock, Bloom
Shock, Stock
Shock, Sound
Shoes, Shoon
Shoes, Boots
Shook, Quook
Shoot, Scoot
Shoot, Sault, Swift
Short, Shorn, Shore
Shout, Spout, Whoop,
   Whoot
Showy, Gaudy
Shred, Scrod
Shrew, Screw, Shrow
Shrub, Shrab
Shuck, Pluck
Shyly, Coyly
Sided, Aided
Siege, Sedge
Sight, Light
Silly, Empty
Silly, Silky, Milky
Silly, Softy
Simar, Cimar, Cymer
Siren, Syren
Sirup, Sirop, Syrup
Sissy, Missy
Skald, Scald
Skate, Scate
Skioy, Skyey
Skiff, Whiff
Skims, Skips, Slips, Flits,
   Flies
Skink, Skunk
Skink, Drink
Skite, Skyte
Skite, Skate
Skulk, Sculk
Slack, Crank
Slade, Glade
Slake, Slime
Slash, Smash
Slate, Slatt, Slats
Sleek, Fleet
Slice, Mince
Slice, Piece
Slice, Carve
Slice, Shave
Slick, Sleek
Slide, Glide
Slimy, Slime
Slink, Slide
Sling, Fling
Sling, Swing
Slish, Slash
Sloid, Sloyd
Slope, Elope
Slope, Slopy
Slops, Shaps, Clats
Slugs, Slogs
Slung, Swung, Flung
Slyly, Slily
Smack, Spank, Spang
Smack, Crack, Clack
Smack, Whack
Smell, Scent
Smelt, Smolt
Smirk, Smile
Smock, Stock, Frock
Smote, Smite
Smout, Smoot
Smout, Smowt, Smolt

Snack, Chack
Snaps, Knaps
Snaps, Slaps
Snaps, Snips, Snigs
Snarl, Gnarl, Gnarr
Sneak, Steal
Sneer, Fleer
Sniff, Snift, Snuff
Snipe, Scape
Snook, Snouk
Snore, Snort
Snort, Sniff
Soils, Fouls
Soggy, Boggy, Moory
Soldi, Soldo
Solid, Valid
Solid, Sound
Sonsy, Soncy
Sordo, Sorda
Sorts, Types
Sorts, Forms
Sough, Cough
Sound, Solid, Valid
Sound, Touch
Sound, Round
Souse, Tease
Souse, Douse, Dowse
South, North, Rhomb
Sower, Mower
Space, Stage
Spade, Slade, Swage,
   Share
Spade, Spado
Spale, Spail
Spale, Spall, Speld
Spall, Spalt
Spang, Sling, Fling
Spank, Smack, Spang
Spare, Scare
Speak, Swear
Spear, Skean
Speck, Fleck
Speed, Breed
Speir, Speer
Speld, Spelk
Speld, Spelt
Spent, Spilt
Spice, Space
Spice, Sauce
Spicy, Spiky
Spies, Spots
Spike, Spick
Spike, Spine, Spile, Spire
Spile, Spill
Spill, Spilt
Spill, Spoil
Spine, Spina, Chine
Spink, Swift
Spiny, Spiky, Spicy
Spirt, Spurt
Spits, Slits
Split, Burst
Spoke, Spake
Spoon, Scoop
Spoon, Spoom
Sposh, Slosh
Spout, Snout
Spout, Shout
Sprat, Sprag
Sprat, Sprod
Sprig, Sprit
Sprig, Spray, Strig

Spurt, Spirt
Squat, Squab
Stack, Stalk
Stack, Shock
Staff, Stave
Staid, Stoic
Stain, Grain
Stake, Stack
Stalk, Stale, Stall
Stalk, Stock
Stall, Stand
Stamp, Stump, Stomp
Stand, Stall
Stank, Stunk
Stare, Start
Stare, Glare
Start, Spurt
State, Stage
State, Scope
Stave, Stake, Trave
Stead, Stand
Stean, Steen, Stein
Steed, Steer, Sheep
Steel, Stone
Steep, Sheer
Steer, Steed, Stote
Stern, Harsh
Stick, Stock
Stick, Staff
Stick, Stuck
Stiff, Stuff
Stilt, Stile
Stime, Styme
Stint, Stent, Stunt
Stint, Spink
Stint, Stilt
Stoat, Shoat, Stote
Stock, Frock, Smock
Stoep, Stoop
Stola, Stole
Stone, Stony
Stook, Stouk
Stook, Shock
Stoop, Stoup
Stoop, Sloop
Stoop, Swoop
Stoop, Stoep
Stoor, Stour
Store, Stock
Storm, Stoor, Stour
Stote, Sheep, Steer, Steed, Whelp
Stout, Stoup
Stout, Proud
Store, Scope
Strap, Thrap
Strap, Strop, Strip
Straw, Strae
Strew, Strow
Strip, Strap, Strop
Strip, Berob
Strip, Strig
Strum, Thrum
Style, Stile
Style, Stole
Suite, Suits
Suits, Writs
Surge, Bulge
Surly, Gurly, Burly
Surly, Sulky
Swage, Slade, Spade
Swale, Slade

Swale, Swang
Swamp, Swang
Swang, Swamp
Sweat, Swelt
Sweer, Sweir
Swift, Shoot
Swift, Sault, Fleet
Swift, Agile, Quick
Swift, Brisk
Swill, Spill, Still
Swops, Chops, Shops
Swore, Sworn
Sylph, Nymph
Sylva, Silva
Taffy, Toffy
Talpa, Salpa
Tamin, Tammy, Tamis
Tapir, Tiger
Tarot, Taroc
Tarry, Delay
Tarve, Curve
Tasks, Taxes
Taste, Tasty, Nasty
Taxes, Rates
Taxed, Rated
Taxes, Tasks
Teach, Peach
Teach, Train
Teach, Coach
Tease, Souse
Tease, Feeze
Teeth, Tooth, Mouth
Tench, Perch
Tends, Fends
Tents, Tests
Tepid, Gelid, Fetid
Tepid, Calid
Terse, Dense
Testy, Techy, Nasty
Testy, Gusty
These, Those, Whose, Whoso
Thing, Being
Think, Opine
Third, Shire
Thrap, Strap
Throw, Threw
Throb, Three
Thrum, Strum
Thuja, Thuya
Thumb, Three
Tiara, Mitre
Tides, Rides
Tiger, Zebra
Tiler, Tyler
Timid, Pavid
Tippy, Tipsy
Tithe, Tythe
Title, Table
Title, Tithe
Toast, Roast, Reast
Toile, Twill
Toile, Voile
Toile, Foule
Toman, Koban
Tooth, Teeth
Tooth, Mouth
Topee, Toque
Topsy, Mopsy, Popsy
Toque, Tuque
Torch, Pitch
Torso, Torse, Corse

Totem, Token
Totty, Dotty
Touch, Sound
Tough, Teugh, Teuch
Tough, Rough
Towed, Rowed
Trace, Track, Tract
Trace, Trave
Trade, Trode
Trade, Trash
Trail, Trawl, Train
Trail, Brail
Train, Trail
Trait, Trace
Tramp, Trant
Tramp, Shack
Tramp, Scamp
Trave, Stave, Stake
Tread, Trend, Troad
Trees, Tares
Tress, Dress
Trick, Frock
Tries, Shies
Trill, Twirl
Trill, Troll
Troll, Brill, Prill
Troll, Trant
Troll, Trawl
Troop, Group, Crowd
Troth, Truth, Sooth
Trout, Troll
Truck, Trunk
Truck, Track
Tubas, Tubae
Tubby, Fubby, Fubsy
Tuile, Foule
Tulip, Oxlip
Tumpy, Humpy, Bumpy
Tutas, Tunas
Tweed, Tweel, Twill
Twill, Drill
Twilt, Quilt
Twirl, Swirl, Whirl
Twirl, Twire
Twirl, Trill
Twist, Twine
Twyer, Tweer, Twier
Types, Tones
Types, Sorts
Umber, Amber
Umiak, Kaiak, Kayak
Unbag, Unbay, Unbar
Unite, Unity, Unify, Amity
Unity, Union
Upbar, Unbar
Urson, Bison, Vison
Usurp, Steal
Vaded, Faded, Jaded
Vague, Loose
Vairy, Hairy
Valve, Valva
Valid, Solid
Vares, Canes, Wands
Vasty, Lusty
Veins, Reins
Veney, Venew
Verge, Marge
Verve, Nerve
Vetch, Fitch, Pitch
Vicar, Vizer
Vifda, Vivda

Villa, Vills
Viola, Viols
Vison, Bison, Vixen, Urson
Visor, Vizor
Vitis, Vitex
Vives, Fives, Hives
Vivid, Nitid
Vixen, Vison, Viper
Vizer, Vicar
Voice, Noise
Voile, Toile
Volta, Polka
Voted, Vowed
Wader, Jager, Eagle
Wages, Miser
Wages, Gages, Games
Waist, Wrist
Wands, Canes, Vares
Wanes, Waxes
Wanes, Bates
Water, Cater
Water, Lager, Latex
Waves, Wares
Waxed, Woxen
Weald, Heath
Weary, Worry
Weary, Heavy
Weeds, Welds
Weedy, Seedy, Needy
Weepy, Seepy
Welsh, Welch
Whack, Smack
Whack, Whang
Whale, Dhole
Whelp, Sheep (see Stote)
Where, There
Which, Whilk
Whiff, Skiff
Whiff, Whale
Whirl, Whorl
Whirl, Twirl, Swirl
Whisk, Whish
White, Whole
Whoop, Whoot
Whose, Whoso
Width, Girth
Wight, Light
Wilds, Hilds
Wilts, Welts
Wince, Dance
Wince, Winch
Wiser, Sager, Saner
Witch, Birch
Withy, Lithe, Lythe
Woman, Women
Wooer, Lover
World, Mould
Worry, Harry
Worse, Worst, Warre
Worst, First
Wound, Pound
Wrath, Wroth
Wrath, Irate
Wreck, Wrack, Break
Wrest, Press
Wrick, Crick
Wrist, Waist
Write, Wrote
Writs, Suits
Xebec, Zebec
Yager, Jager

Yapon, Yupon
Yards, Hands
Yawls, Yowls, Bawls
Yield, Leave
Yield, Waive
Yodel, Jodel, Yodle
Yokes, Yokel
Youth, Young
Zebec, Xebec
Zebra, Tiger
Zibet, Bidet, Civet
Zorro, Zorra, Burro, Goral

6 Letters

Abduce, Abduct
Abjure, Adjure
Abkary, Abkari
Abrade, Scrape
Abrupt, Obtuse
Accede, Accept
Accrue, Accrew
Action, Motion
Adhere, Cohere, Inhere
Adieus, Adieux
Adorer, Amoret
Adorer, Adored
Advise, Advice
Affair, Effeir, Effere
Affair, Affect
Aflame, Ablaze
Affray, Effray
Afraid, Afeard
Agazed, Amazed
Agouti, Agouta
Aileen, Eileen
Ailing, Pining
Aiming, Timing, Arming
Airman, Airmen
Amends, Amende
Amends, Emends
Amerce, Amende
Anadem, Diadem
Anatta, Anatto
Angels, Ariels
Angora, Angola
Annual, Manual
Apiary, Aviary
Arcade, Parade
Ardent, Intent, Eident, Watery
Argute, Astute
Armlet, Anklet
Aroint, Aroynt
Ascent, Ascend
Ashlar, Ashler
Aslant, Askant
Aspect, Direct
Assess, Assize
Assure, Insure, Ensure
Astart, Astert
Astute, Spruce
Attach, Stitch
Attain, Obtain
Attest, Obtest
Atween, Atwixt
August, Autumn
Avoset, Avocet
Babble, Gabble, Rabble
Baboon, Racoon
Backet (see Basket)

Backer, Banker
Badger, Pester
Badger, Ranger
Baffle, Maffle
Baling, Saving
Ballot, Bullet
Banana, Batata, Potato, Tomato
Banana, Samara
Banana, Panada
Banged, Barged
Banian, Banyan
Banner, Fannel
Banter, Tatter
Barbel, Turbot, Burbot
Barely, Rarely, Hardly
Barely, Merely
Barley, Parley
Barmen, Batmen
Barque, Marque
Barque, Caique
Barras, Jarrah, Marram
Barred, Hinged
Barred, Banned
Barrel, Corral, Korral
Barret, Berret
Bashed, Basted
Basket, Casket, Wisket, Backet, Bucket
Basket, Packet, Jacket
Basses, Bassos
Basset, Messin
Basted, Bashed
Batlet, Mallet
Bathed, Washed
Bating, Saving
Batten, Fatten, Battel
Batter, Hatter
Batter, Butter, Bitter
Batter, Patter
Baubee, Bawbee
Bauble, Bawble
Beachy, Pebbly
Beadle, Beagle
Bearer, Wearer
Beaten, Bested
Beaver, Boater
Become, Became
Become, Behove
Bedlam, Madman
Beeves, Calves
Beetle, Pestle
Before, Tofore
Befoul, Defoul
Behalf, Behoof
Behind, Beyond
Belies, Denies
Bemean, Demean
Bertha, Berthe
Berths, Births
Bertie, Gertie
Betray, Bewray
Betide, Betime
Bettor, Better
Bewail, Beweep
Bezant, Byzant
Bigamy, Digamy
Bilker, Bulker
Binate, Binary
Blanch, Blench, Bleach
Blared, Roared
Blench, Flinch

Blouse, Blowse
Bodger, Monger
Bogies, Bogles
Bombax, Bombyx, Bombic
Boodle, Noodle, Doodle
Borage, Lovage
Bother, Pother, Dither
Bottle, Pottle, Kettle
Bounce, Pounce
Bowler, Boater
Brasen, Brazen
Brayer, Grater, Graver
Breach, Broach
Breese, Breeze
Breton, Briton, Triton
Bridle, Saddle
Briony, Bryony
Brogue, Brogan
Broker, Grocer
Bubble, Hubble
Buffer, Duffer
Bugles, Buglet
Bulged, Bagged
Bullet, Pellet, Ballet
Bumble, Humble
Bummer, Bummle
Bundle, Boodle
Bungle, Wuzzle, Jumble
Bungle, Boggle
Bunted, Butted
Burrow, Furrow
Bursar, Purser
Bustle, Justle, Jostle, Hustle, Rustle
Butler, Sutler
Butter, Batter
Byname, Toname
Cabana, Havana
Cabman, Carman
Cabrit, Cabrie
Cadger, Codger
Caesar, Kaiser
Caftan, Kaftan
Caiman, Cayman
Caique, Barque
Calces, Calxes
Calker, Calkin
Calker, Cawker
Calves, Beeves
Camera, Kamera
Camise, Camese
Canada, Canaan
Cancel, Repeal
Cancer, Canker
Candle, Kindle
Canned, Tinned
Cannel, Candle
Cannon, Falcon
Cantel, Cantle
Canter, Career
Canton, Canyon
Canuck, Kanuck
Capote, Mantle
Carfax, Carfox
Carrot, Yarrow, Marrow
Carter, Porter
Carton, Carboy
Carved, Carven
Caster, Castor
Casket (see Basket)

Casque, Masque
Cation, Kation
Caused, Raised
Cavass, Kavass
Cavern, Casern
Ceases, Leaves
Celtic, Keltic
Cental, Cantar
Centre, Center
Ceroon, Seroon
Change, Chance
Chants, Chanty
Chanty, Shanty
Cheery, Cherry
Chevin, Cheven
Chisil, Chesil
Choose, Choice
Chuffs, Churls
Cicada, Cicala, Cigala
Cinder, Tinder
Cinema, Kinema
Circle, Cirque, Circus
Circle, Virole
Citric, Nitric, Picric
Cleans, Clears
Clench, Clinch, Clutch
Clergy, Clerks
Clique, Claque
Cloudy, Gloomy
Clover, Flower
Clumsy, Clumpy
Coarse, Hoarse
Cobalt, Kobalt
Cobles, Cables
Codded, Podded
Coddle, Cuddle, Pettle, Tiddle
Cogent, Potent
Cogged, Cooked
Cohere, Inhere, Adhere
Colder, Cooler
Collar, Collet
Collar, Halter
Column, Pillar
Comely, Lovely
Commit, Submit
Congee, Conjee
Conger, Conner
Confit, Comfit
Cooly, Coldly
Cooper, Hooper
Copeck, Kopeck
Copier, Copyer
Copper, Coffer, Coffin
Corker, Korkir
Corpse, Corpus
Corral, Korral, Barrel
Corvet, Curvet
Cosier, Cozier, Hosier
Cosily, Easily
Cosmos, Kosmos
Coster, Poster
Coster, Couter
Cottar, Cotter
Couple, Double
Couter, Coster
Coward, Dotard
Cowdie, Cowrie
Craggy, Snaggy
Craved, Prayed
Creach, Creagh
Creese, Crease

Crummy, Crumby, Crusty, Crumpy
Crunch, Cranch
Cruset, Cruses, Crusie
Cumber, Hamper
Cummer, Kimmer
Curari, Curara
Curled, Curved
Curred, Purred
Cutter, Putter
Cymoid, Cymose, Cymous
Cymbal, Timbal
Cypher, Cipher, Sypher
Dabble, Jabble
Dacker, Daiker
Dacoit, Dakoit
Dander, Wander
Dander, Fondle
Dander, Temper
Dandle, Fondle
Danish, Danisk
Darken, Darkle
Dasher, Masher
Daubed, Dabbed, Gaumed
Dautie, Dawtie
Dawdle, Daddle, Daidle, Toddle
Dayfly, Mayfly, Gadfly, Dryfly
Deaden, Deafen, Leaden
Decade, Decads
Decide, Define, Desire, Desine
Deckle (see Sickle)
Defame, Deface
Define, Refine
Define, Denote
Defoul, Befoul
Deftly, Deffly
Degree, Decree
Deject, Reject
Delice, Deluce
Delude, Illude
Demean, Bemean
Demise, Devise
Demits, Remits
Denies, Belies
Denote, Devote
Dental, Mental
Dentil, Dentel
Depart, Repair, Desert
Depart, Repart
Depend, Impend
Depict, Design
Depose, Depone
Depute, Repute
Dermal, Dermic
Desert, Depart, Repair
Desert, Desart
Design, Belief, Notion
Design, Result, Effect
Detail, Retail
Detain, Retain, Remain
Detort, Extort
Devise, Device, Design
Diadem, Anadem
Dibble, Dibber
Dibble, Wimple
Digamy, Bigamy
Dimple, Pimple
Dindle, Dinnle
Dingle, Dimple

Dinghy, Dingey
Dinnle, Tingle
Dipper, Nipper, Ripper
Direct, Aspect
Discus, Discal
Dismay, Dismal
Dither, Bother, Pother
Divert, Revert
Divest, Devest
Docile, Facile
Docket, Cocket
Doctor, Rector
Dodged, Cogged
Dodged, Hedged
Dogger, Lugger, Nugger
Doings, Goings
Dollop, Dallop
Domain, Demain
Donald, Ronald
Donkey, Monkey
Doodle, Noodle, Boodle
Dorsal, Tergal
Dossal, Dossel, Missal
Dotage, Nonage
Dotard, Coward
Doting, Loving
Double, Couple
Douser, Douter
Douter, Douser
Drivel, Slaver
Driver, Drover
Drudge, Trudge
Drupel, Drupes
Dryfly, Mayfly, Dayfly,
    Gadfly
Dubber, Dupper
Duffer, Buffer
Duiker, Duyker
Dumose, Dumous
Dunker, Tunker
Dunlin, Puffin
Durdum, Dirdum
Durian, Durion
Dzeron, Dzeren
Eadish, Eddish
Eaglet, Haglet
Earcap, Earlap
Earing, Spring, String
Easily, Cosily
Easter, Eassel
Edward, Howard
Effeir, Affair, Effere
Effray, Affray
Egging, Edging, Urging
Eileen, Aileen
Elfish, Elvish
Embace, Embase
Embalm, Imbalm
Embark, Imbark
Embody, Imbody
Embrue, Imbrue
Emends, Amends
Emmesh, Enmesh
Emmove, Enmove
Empire, Empery
Empusa, Empuse
Encase, Encage
Endite, Indite
Enfest, Infest
Enfold, Infold
Engulf, Ingulf
Enisle, Inisle

Enlock, Inlock
Enmove, Emmove
Enmure, Immure
Ensoul, Insoul
Ensure, Insure, Assure
Entice, Induce
Enwall, Inwall
Enwind, Inwind
Enwrap, Inwrap
Eparch, Exarch
Epodes, Exodes
Eringo, Eryngo
Errant, Erring
Errors, Errata
Excide, Excise
Excite, Incite
Expend, Extend, Extent
Expire, Expiry
Extend, Extent
Extort, Detort
Eyelid, Eyepit
Fabian, Zabian
Fabler, Fibber
Facile, Docile
Facula, Macula
Fading, Lading
Fagend, Tagend
Fagged, Failed
Fannel, Banner
Fardel, Parcel
Faster, Hasten
Father, Mother
Fatten, Batten, Battel
Faunas, Faunae
Feared, Scared
Featly, Neatly
Fecial, Fetial
Feeble, Flabby
Fellow, Person
Fellow, Follow
Fenced, Penned
Fennec, Ferret, Vervet
Ferrel, Verrel
Ferret, Vervet, Fennec
Fetish, Fetich
Fetter, Tether
Fettle, Settle
Fickle, Tickle
Fiddle, Faddle
Fiddle, Tiddle, Piddle
Finder, Winder
Findon, Finnan
Finely, Nicely
Finest, Nicest
Finger, Tongue
Fisgig, Fizgig
Fishes, Pisces
Flabby, Flaccy, Flaggy
Flagon, Flacon
Flange, Flanch
Flench, Flinch, Flense
Flimsy, Slimsy
Flinch, Blench
Flitted, Flirted
Florid, Flashy
Flouse, Floush
Flower, Clover
Foemen, Yeomen
Foiled, Fooled
Fondle, Dandle
Footle, Foozle
Formal, Normal

Formed, Forced, Forged
Forpit, Forpet
Fosset, Faucet
Foster, Sister
Fowler, Bowler
Fraise, Froise
Frenzy, Franzy
Friary, Priory
Frieze, Fringe
Frowsy, Frowzy
Frozen, Froren
Frumpy, Grumpy
Fuddle, Muddle
Fuller, Muller
Fumble, Mumble
Funnel, Tunnel
Funnel, Fummel
Furrow, Burrow
Gabble, Babble, Gaggle
Gabble, Garble
Gadfly (see Dayfly)
Gaelic, Gallic
Gaffer, Gammer, Ganger,
    Ranger
Gaggle, Gabble, Cackle
Gaiety, Gayety
Galore, Golore
Galosh, Golosh, Galage
Gambet, Gannet, Gander
Ganger, Ranger (see
    Gaffer)
Gannet, Lannor
Gaoler, Jailor, Jailer
Gargle, Gurgle, Guggle
Garial, Gavial
Garner, Gather
Garnet, Jasper
Garran, Garron
Garter, Gaiter
Gashed, Lashed
Gasket, Lasket, Gaskin
Gaumed, Daubed, Dabbed
Gaupus, Gawpus
Genial, Xenial, Jovial
Gennet, Jennet, Ginnet
Gentle, Semple, Simple
Gerent, Regent
Gerald, Gerard
Gertie, Bertie
Gharri, Gharry
Gheber, Ghebre, Guebre,
    Gueber
Gimbel, Gimmal
Gingal, Jingal
Gingko, Ginkgo
Girdle, Kirtle
Glassy, Glossy
Gloomy, Cloudy
Gluten, Glutin
Goblet, Goglet
Goings, Doings
Gomuti, Gomuto
Gossan, Gozzan
Gothic, Sothic
Grater, Graver, Brayer
Grates, Grides, Graves
Grease, Greasy
Greeve, Grieve
Greeve, Greave, Grieve
Grilse, Grouse
Grocer, Glover, Broker
Grouse, Grouce

Grumpy, Frumpy
Grumpy, Glumpy
Guggle, Gurgle, Gargle
Hackle (see Sickle)
Hackle, Heckle
Haggle, Mangle
Haggle, Higgie
Haglet, Eaglet
Halloo, Halloa
Halter, Collar
Halter, Halser, Hawser
Hamate, Hamous, Hamose
Hammam, Hummum
Hammer, Rammer
Hamper, Hinder
Hamper, Cumber
Handle, Famble
Handle, Manage
Hanger, Hanjar
Hanker, Hunger
Hankle, Tangle
Harmed, Marred
Hasten, Hasted
Hasten, Faster
Hatter, Natter, Batter
Haunch, Paunch
Havana, Cabana
Hawker, Pedlar
Health, Wealth, Wholth
Heaped, Reaped
Heckle (see Sickle)
Hedged, Dodged
Hegira, Hejira
Helped, Holpen
Herden, Harden, Hurden
Hoarse, Coarse
Hobble, Wobble
Hockey, Hookey
Hoddle, Toddle
Homely, Comely, Lovely
Honest, Modest
Hoodoo, Voodoo
Hooker, Howker
Hooper, Cooper
Hoopoo, Hoopoe
Hopper, Copper
Horded, Herded
Horror, Terror
Hosier, Cosier, Cozier
Houdah, Howdah
Howard, Edward
Howker, Hooker
Hoyden, Hoiden
Hubble, Bubble
Hubbub, Hubble
Huddle, Muddle
Humble, Bumble
Humble, Tumble
Hunger, Hanker
Hunted, Wanted
Hunter, Hunger
Hurdle, Wattle
Hurrah, Hurray
Hustle, Hurtle
Idolon, Idolum
Illude, Delude
Imbalm, Embalm
Imbody, Embody
Imbark, Embark
Impart, Import
Impend, Depend

Impone, Impose
Import, Impart
Impost, Import
Impugn, Repugn
Incite, Invite, Indite
Incite, Excite
Infect, Inject
Inflow, Influx
Inhere, Cohero, Adhere
Injury, Injure
Inlock, Enlock
Insure, Ensure, Assure
Intent, Ardent, Watery
Intent, Intend
Invite, Indite, Invoke
Iodine, Iodide, Iodate
Isabel, Isobel, Ishbel
Jabble, Dabble
Jackal, Shakal
Jacket, Rocket
Jagged, Ragged, Rugged
Jagger, Yagger
Jailor, Jailer, Gaoler
Jarrah, Barras, Marram
Jasper, Garnet
Jennet, Gennet, Ginnet
Jersey, Kersey
Jetsam, Jetsom, Jetson
Jigsaw, Pitsaw
Jingle, Jangle
Jingal, Gingal
Jogged, Jolted
Jostle, Hustle, Bustle, Rustle
Jovial, Genial, Xenial
Jowder, Jowter
Joyous, Joyful
Jumble, Wuzzle, Bungle
Junket, Sunket
Kaiser, Caesar
Kamera, Camera
Kamila, Kamela
Kation, Cation
Kavass, Cavass
Kelter, Kilter
Kettle, Bottle, Pottle
Kiblah, Keblah
Kiddle, Kettle
Kindle, Candle
Kirtle, Girdle
Kronen, Kroner
Korral, Corral, Barrel
Lading, Laving
Lading, Fading
Lanary, Panary
Lanner, Gannet
Lanner, Linnet
Larder, Pantry
Larger, Longer
Lashed, Gashed, Rashed
Lasses, Passes, Misses
Lasses, Ladies
Latent, Secret
Lavers, Liners
Leaden, Deafen
Leaped, Lepped
Leaves, Leases
Leaves, Ceases
Lector, Rector
Ledger, Leiger
Ledger, Lodger
Lemuel, Samuel

Lilacs, Lilies
Lineal, Linear
Linger, Loiter
Linget, Lingot
Linnet, Lanner
Linsey, Winsey, Wincey
Lintel, Mantle
Lionel, Lionet
Lipped, Lisped
Little, Tittle, Leetle
Lively, Lovely
Locate, Locale
Locket, Locker
Lodger, Ledger
Loiter, Linger, Potter
Lordly, Portly
Loriot, Parrot
Lotion, Potion
Lovage, Borage
Lovely, Comely, Homely
Lovely, Likely
Loving, Doting
Lugged, Tugged, Rugged
Lugger, Nugger, Dogger
Lumber, Cumber
Lumber, Timber
Lurdan, Lurden
Macula, Macule, Mackle
Macula, Facula
Madcap, Maniac, Madman
Madman, Bedlam
Maffle, Baffle
Maggie, Margie
Magilp, Megilp
Magnet, Magnes
Maigre, Maugre
Malkin, Maukin
Mallet, Batlet
Mallet, Pallet
Mammet, Maumet, Mawmet
Manage, Handle
Manage, Manege, Menage
Mangle, Haggle
Manner, Tender
Mantle, Lintel
Mantle, Capote
Mantle, Manton, Mantua
Manual, Annual
Margay, Margot
Marmot, Margay
Marone, Maroon
Marone, Morone
Marque, Barque
Marred, Marked
Marram, Jarrah, Barras
Marred, Maimed
Marrow, Carrot, Yarrow, Marram
Martin, Merlin, Marten
Masher, Dasher
Masque, Casque
Master, Mister, Pastor
Matron, Patron
Mayfly (see Dayfly)
Medial, Median, Mesian, Mesial
Mediar, Poplar
Medley, Motley
Melody, Monody
Melted, Molten

Mental, Dental
Method, Manner
Minnie, Winnie, Binnie
Minter, Monier
Missal, Dossal, Dossel
Missed, Misled
Misses, Passes, Lasses
Missis, Missus, Misses
Mistle, Mizzle, Missel
Modest, Honest
Mohawk, Mohock
Mollah, Mullah, Moolah
Moloch, Molech
Monkey, Donkey
Monday, Sunday
Monger, Bodger
Morale, Morals
Morsel, Parcel
Moslem, Muslim
Mother, Father
Motile, Mobile
Motion, Action
Muckle, Mickle
Muddle, Fuddle
Muddle, Huddle
Muddle, Muzzle
Muffle, Mumble
Muller, Fuller
Mumble, Rumble
Muscle, Mussel
Mutiny, Mutine
Muzzle, Mistle
Napkin, Nankin
Natant, Naiant, Nayant
Nation, Family
Nearly, Nearby
Neatly, Featly
Nestor, Mentor
Nettle, Rattle
Nicely, Finely
Nicest, Finest
Nicher, Nicker
Nicker, Pecker, Yucker
Nickle, Tickey
Nimble, Wimble
Nipper, Dipper, Dopper
Nipper, Kipper
Nonage, Dotage
Noodle, Boodle, Doodle
Notion, Belief
Nought, Naught
Nugger, Dogger, Lugger
Nuzzle, Nousle, Nestle
Object, Obtest
Obtain, Attain
Obtest, Attest
Obtund, Obtuse
Obtund, Retund
Obtuse, Abrupt
Ondine, Undine
Orchid, Orchis
Oroide, Oreide
Ortive, Orient
Oswald, Oswold
Oulong, Oolong
Outbid, Outdid
Outwit, Outvie
Overdo, Overgo
Oxgang, Oxland, Oxgate
Packet, Parcel, Fardel
Padded, Wadded
Paddle, Pattle

Paddle, Waddle
Pagoda, Pagode
Painim, Paynim
Paints, Prints
Palace, Castle
Pallet, Mallet
Panada, Banana
Pandit, Pundit
Panton, Wanton
Pantry, Panary, Lanary
Pantry, Larder
Papuan, Papuas
Parade, Arcade
Parcel, Morsel
Parian, Pariah
Parker, Warder, Warden
Parley, Barley
Parrot, Loriot
Parson, Pastor
Passes, Misses, Lasses
Pasted, Posted
Pastel, Pastil
Pastor, Parson
Pastor, Parrot
Patter, Batter
Paunch, Haunch
Pavior, Pavier
Peacod, Peapod
Pebble, Cobble, Rubble
Pebble, Coggle
Pebbly, Beachy
Pecker, Nicker, Yucker
Pedler, Pedlar
Pedlar, Hawker
Pellet, Tablet
Pengun, Popgun
Penned, Fenced
Peplum, Peplus
Perkin, Parkin
Person, Fellow
Person, Parson
Pester, Fester, Badger
Pestle, Beetle
Pettle (see Coddle)
Pewter, Potter
Picket, Piquet
Picric, Citric, Nitric
Pigeon, Wigeon
Piggin, Pipkin
Piggin, Noggin
Piling, Paling
Pillar, Column
Pilled, Rifled
Pilule, Pilula
Pimple, Dimple, Wimple
Pinder, Pinner
Pining, Ailing
Pinned, Penned
Piping, Pining
Pipped, Peeped
Pisces, Fishes
Pitsaw, Jigsaw
Plaise, Plaice
Planes, Planer
Planes, Planet
Plough, Pleugh
Pocket, Locket, Locker,
   Socket
Podde l, Codded
Polite, Polish
Pommel, Pummel
Poplar, Medlar

Poppet, Puppet
Porous, Porose
Porter, Carter, Potter
Portly, Lordly
Posnet, Posset
Potash, Potass
Potato, Tomato, Batata,
   Banana, Samara
Potent, Cogent
Potion, Lotion
Pother, Potter
Pother, Bother, Dither
Potter, Linger, Loiter
Pottle, Bottle, Kettle
Pounce, Bounce, Source
Powter, Pouter
Powwow, Pawwaw
Prayed, Craved
Preace, Prease
Premus, Primal
Priory, Friary
Proved, Proven
Proved, Groped, Probed
Puffin, Dunlin
Pulwar, Palwar
Purred, Purled
Purred, Curred
Purser, Bursar
Pushto, Pushtu
Putted, Potted
Putter, Cutter
Puttie, Puttee
Pyjama, Pajama
Quaint, Queint
Quaker, Shaker
Quaver, Quiver
Quinch, Quitch
Quiver, Shiver
Rabble, Babble, Gabble
Racoon, Baboon
Raddle, Reddle, Ruddle
Radius, Radian
Raffia, Raphia
Rafted, Wafted
Ragged, Rugged, Jagged
Raised, Roused
Raised, Caused
Raises, Rouses, Rousts
Ramble, Stroll
Rammer, Hammer
Ranged, Ranked
Ranger, Badger
Ranger, Ranker (see
   Gaffer)
Rarely, Barely, Hardly
Rashed, Gashed, Lashed
Rasure, Razure
Rattat, Rattan
Ratter, Setter
Rattle, Nettle
Rattle, Tattle
Raving, Roving
Really, Verily
Realty, Fealty
Reaped, Heaped
Reared, Raised
Rearer, Raiser
Rebate, Rabate
Rebuff, Rebuke
Rebuke, Refute, Refuse
Recall, Recant
Recede, Secede

Recoil, Recule, Recuil, Resile
Reckon, Reason
Record, Report, Reword
Rector, Doctor
Rector, Lector
Reebok, Rhebok
Refine, Define
Reflux, Reflow
Reform, Resort
Refuse, Recuse, Refute
Regard, Reward
Regard, Remark
Regent, Gerent
Regina, Regent
Reject, Deject
Relate, Delate
Relate, Recite
Relive, Revive, Regive
Remedy, Remede
Remits, Demits
Remove, Remble, Remedy
Remove, Serene
Render, Tender
Rennet, Runnet
Repair, Depart, Desert
Repeal, Cancel
Repeat, Revert
Repeck, Ripeck, Rypeck
Repent, Relent
Repent, Regret
Report, Renown
Report, Retort, Return
Repose, Depose
Repugn, Impugn
Repute, Depute
Reseal, Reseat, Reseam
Rested, Seated
Result, Design, Effect
Retain, Detain, Remain
Retail, Detail
Retard, Retain
Retell, Retail
Retire, Recede, Resile
Retire, Resign
Retund, Obtund
Return, Retort, Revert
Return, Retire
Revert, Revest
Revert, Divert
Review, Revise
Ridged, Rugged
Rifled, Pilled
Rigour, Vigour
Ringer, Ranger
Roared, Blared
Rockel, Rochet
Rockel, Jacket
Rocker, Roller
Romany, Nomade
Ronald, Donald
Ronion, Ronyon
Rootle, Rookle
Rosery, Rosary
Rotten, Rotted
Rouble, Double
Rowing, Rating
Rubble, Pebble
Rueful, Woeful, Waeful
Rugate, Rugose, Rugous
Ruffle, Runkle

Ruffle, Rustle, Rumple
Rugged, Ragged, Jagged
Rugged, Shaggy
Rugous, Rugose, Rugate
Rumble, Mumble
Rumble, Tumble
Rumple, Rimple, Ruffle
Runlet, Runnel
Rupert, Hubert, Robert
Rustle, Fissle
Sabian, Zabian
Sachel, Sachet
Sadden, Harden
Saddle, Bridle
Safest, Surest
Saggar, Sagger
Saguin, Sagoin
Sailor, Sailer
Sailor, Tailor, Jailor
Saline, Salina
Sallow, Yellow, Fallow, Mellow
Sallow, Willow, Tallow, Mallow
Salter, Soutar, Souter, Sowter
Salute, Salewe
Salver, Waiter
Samara, Banana
Sambur, Samboo
Samuel, Lemuel
Sander, Zander
Sandix, Sandyx
Sannup, Sannop
Sanpan, Sampan
Santir, Santur
Sargus, Saurus
Sarlac, Sarlak, Sarlyk
Saving, Bating
Scarce, Scanty, Sparse
Scared, Feared
Scheme, Schema
Scovel, Shovel
Scrape, Abrade
Scream, Screak, Shriek
Scribe, Scrive
Scruff, Skruff
Scurfy, Scurvy
Scurry, Skurry, Flurry
Seadog, Seahog
Seated, Stated
Seated, Rested
Secede, Secern
Secede, Recede
Secret, Latent
Sedent, Silent
Seisin, Seizin
Sennit, Sinnet
Senora, Senors
Septet, Sestet, Sextet
Serene, Remove
Serene, Sedate
Seriph, Ceriph
Seroon, Ceroon
Server, Verger
Sestet, Sextet, Septet
Setter, Ratter
Settle, Fettle
Settle, Settee
Shabby, Scabby
Shaggy, Rugged
Shakal, Jackal

Shaker, Quaker
Shanty, Stable
Shanty, Chanty
Shaped, Shapen
Shaved, Shaven
Shaver, Shiver, Sliver
Shears, Sheers
Sherry, Wherry
Sheugh, Sheuch
Shindy, Shinny, Shinty
Shirts, Skirts, Shorts, Skilts, Shifts
Shiver, Skiver
Shiver, Quiver
Shovel, Trowel
Shrank, Shrunk
Shriek, Shrike
Shrine, Scrine
Sickle, Tackle, Hackle, Deckle, Heckle
Sicsac, Ziczac
Silvan, Sylvan
Silver, Gilder
Simple, Gentle, Semple
Simple, Single
Single, Singly, Simply, Solely
Sipple, Tipple
Sirdar, Sircar, Sirkar
Sister, Foster
Slaves, Slaver, Slaved, Slavey
Slaver, Drivel
Sledge, Sleigh
Sleezy, Sleazy
Slides, Slopes
Slimsy, Flimsy
Slushy, Sloshy, Slashy, Sposhy
Smithy, Smiddy, Stithy
Smudge, Sludge
Snaggy, Craggy
Snatch, Scatch
Soaked, Sopped
Soccer, Socker
Socket (see Pocket)
Sonsie, Soncie
Sopped, Soaked, Seeped
Sorter, Porter
Sothic, Gothic
Soujee, Soojee
Source, Bounce, Pounce
Sowans, Sowens
Splint, Splent
Sponge, Spunge
Sposhy, Sloshy
Spotty, Smutty
Sprain, Strain
Sprang, Sprung, Sprong
Spring, Sprint
Sprint, Sprent
Sprout, Sprunt
Spruce, Astute
Spruce, Rankle
Squall, Squeak, Squeal, Squawk
Square, Squire
Staple, Stable
Starve, Sterve
Stayed, Staved
Steady, Stable
Stingy, Stinty

Stipes, Stalls
Stitch, Attach
Strake, Stroke, Strike
Stored, Stowed
Strafe, Strike
Strain, Sprain
Strain, Strait
Strand, Strond
Stream, Streak
Street, Strayt
Strich, Strick
Strict, Strait
Stride, Stryde
Strike, Stroke
Strike, Strife, Strive
Strike, Strafe
Stroll, Ramble
Stumpy, Stubby, Stuggy
Stupid, Stolid
Submit, Commit
Sucker, Sucket
Suckle, Nuzzle, Nestle, Nousle
Sullen, Solein, Solemn
Sultan, Soldan
Sunday, Monday
Sunder, Sundry
Sunket, Junket
Sunned, Sonned
Swarth, Wraith
Swerve, Swarve
Tabard, Taberd
Tablet, Pellet
Tablet, Tables
Tackle (see Sickle)
Tackle, Tickle
Tagend, Fagend
Tailor, Tailer
Tallot, Tallat, Tallet
Tambac, Tombac
Tamine, Taminy, Tamise
Taintam, Tomtom, Tumtum
Tangle, Hankle
Tanjib, Tanzib
Tanner, Tenner
Tanrec, Tenrec
Tarpan, Garran, Garron
Tarpon, Tarpum
Tasted, Tested
Taslet, Tasset
Tatter, Banter
Taupie, Tawpie
Tauten, Fasten
Tautie, Tawtie
Teapot, Teapoy, Teacup
Teasel, Teazel, Teazle
Temper, Pamper
Tender, Render
Tender, Manner
Tender, Tenter
Tergal, Dorsal
Terret, Territ
Terror, Horror
Tester, Taster, Tenter
Tetchy, Touchy
Tether, Fetter
Thatch, Thetch
Themes, Theses
Thirst, Thrust, Thrist
Thrash, Thresh
Thrash, Thwack

Threep, Threap
Throat, Thorax
Throbs, Throes
Tickey, Nickle
Tilted, Tipped
Timbal, Cymbal
Timbal, Tymbal
Timber, Lumber
Tincal, Tinkal
Tinder, Cinder
Tingle, Tangle
Tingle, Dinnle
Tingle, Tinkle
Tinker, Tinner
Tinned, Canned
Tinted, Tinged
Tipped, Tapped
Tipped, Tilted
Tipple, Sipple
Titbit, Tidbit
Toddle, Daddle
Toffee, Coffee
Tofore, Before
Tomato (see Potato)
Tomcat, Ramcat, Wombat
Toname, Byname
Tongue, Tonsil
Tongue, Finger
Tooart, Tewart
Tophat, Pothat
Toupee, Toupet
Trapan, Trepan
Treble, Triple
Trebly, Triply
Trevet, Trivet
Trigly, Trimly, Primly
Tripod, Tripos
Triton, Briton, Breton
Trowel, Shovel
Tugged, Lugged, Rugged
Tumble, Jumble, Rumble
Tunker, Dunker
Tunnel, Funnel
Turbot, Burbot, Barbel
Turner, Turney
Turret, Garret
Umbril, Umbrel
Unfirm, Infirm
Unfold, Unbolt, Unhold
Unheal, Unhele
Unlock, Unbolt
Unpack, Unpick
Unroot, Uproot
Urging, Urgent (see Egging)
Utmost, Upmost
Valkyr, Walkyr
Varvel, Vervel
Velvet, Vellet,
Vendor, Vender
Verger, Server
Verily, Really
Verrel, Ferrel
Vervet, Ferret, Fennec
Vesper, Hesper
Vigour, Rigour
Virole, Circle
Virous, Virose
Vizier, Wizier
Voodoo, Vaudoo, Voudoo
Voodoo, Hoodoo

Wabbly, Wobbly
Wadded, Padded
Waddle, Paddle
Wafted, Rafted
Waggle, Wiggle
Waiter, Salver
Waiter, Writer
Walkyr, Valkyr
Wander, Dander
Wanted, Hunted
Warder, Warden, Parker
Warely, Warily
Washed, Bathed
Wastes, Passes
Watery, Ardent, Intent, Eident
Waught, Waucht
Wattle, Hurdle
Wearer, Bearer
Weasel, Weazel, Beaver
Welded, Wedded
Wherry, Sherry
Whatna, Whaten
Wholth, Wealth, Health
Wicker, Wicken
Wicket, Picket
Wigeon, Pigeon
Willow, Sallow, Tallow
Wimple, Dibble
Wincey, Winsey, Linsey
Windle, Bundle, Bandle
Wincey, Winsey, Linsey
Wisket (see Basket)
Wivern, Wyvern
Wizard, Wisard
Wobble, Hobble
Wobble, Wabble
Woeful, Waeful, Rueful
Wonder, Ponder
Wraith, Swarth
Wuzzle, Huddle, Muddle
Xenial, Genial
Xystos, Xystus
Yagger, Jagger
Yankie, Yankee
Yarrow, Marrow, Carrot
Yauped, Yapped, Yelped
Yawled, Bawled, Wawled, Called, Hailed, Wailed
Yellow, Sallow, Fallow
Yeomen, Foemen
Yucker, Pecker, Nicker
Zabian, Fabian
Zaffre, Zaffer
Zander, Sander
Zarape, Serape
Zeraba, Zareba
Zigzag, Wigwag
Zither, Cither

7 Letters

Abasing, Abusing
Abettor, Abetter
Abysmal, Abyssal
Account, Accompt
Acolyte, Acolyth
Acquest, Acquist
Addable, Addible
Adeline, Adaline
Admiral, Ammiral

Adenoid, Adenous
Alchemy, Alchymy
Alumina, Alumine
Amongst, Emongst
Ancient, Antient
Andiron, Endiron
Annatto, Arnotto
Appeach, Impeach
Appoint, Destine
Apprise, Apprize
Assegai, Assegay, Assagai
Assiege, Besiege
Assuage, Asswage
Atropia, Atropin
Aureola, Aureole
Baccare, Backare
Baggage, Luggage
Bandage, Bandeau
Bandbox, Sandbox
Bandles, Bundles
Bandore, Pandore, Pandura
Baneful, Baleful
Bannock, Jannock
Banting, Fasting
Barrier, Barrage
Basenet, Basinet
Bearish, Boarish, Boorish
Bedouin, Bedawin
Becomes, Behoves
Bemazed, Bemused
Bengals, Bengali
Bequest, Request
Besiege, Assiege
Bespeed, Bestead
Biffins, Muffins
Biffins, Piffins
Billion, Million
Blatter, Clatter, Chatter
Blether, Blather
Blesses, Pleases
Blinder, Blinker
Blunket, Blonket
Bluster, Fluster
Bluster, Blatter
Boggard, Boggart
Booster, Boaster
Boscage, Boskage
Boulder, Bowlder
Bounced, Bounded
Bounder, Bouncer
Brahman, Brahmin
Brangle, Wrangle
Branced, Pranced
Bravery, Bravura
Brittle, Bruckle, Brickle
Brittle, Fragile
Brocage, Brokage
Brocket, Pricket
Bromate, Bromine
Buckram, Lockram
Bumboat, Tugboat, Gunboat
Bundles, Bunches
Bundles, Bandles
Bureaus, Bureaux
Burnish, Furnish, Furbish
Burdock, Hardock, Harlock
Bustard, Buzzard
Bustler, Hustler, Rustler, Justler

Butlery, Buttery
Butlery, Sutlery
Cacique, Cazique
Cacodyl, Kacodyl
Cajuput, Cajeput
Calcium, Cadmium
Calends, Kalends
Caliber, Calibre
Caltrop, Caltrap
Campion, Rampion
Cantred, Hundred
Capital, Capitan
Capitol, Capital
Captive, Caitive
Carauna, Caranna
Carcake, Oatcake, Pancake
Careful, Wareful
Cariama, Seriema
Cariboo, Caribou
Caromel, Caramel
Cassock, Hassock
Catchup, Ketchup
Catling, Fatling
Ceramic, Keramic
Certify, Testify
Champac, Champak
Chancre, Shanker
Channel, Chamfer
Charles, Charley
Charlie, Charley
Chatter, Clutter, Clitter, Clatter
Chicory, Succory
Chortle, Chuckle
Chutnee, Chutney
Cithern, Cittern, Zithern, Gittern
Clatter, Blatter
Clitter, Clatter, Clutter
Clobber, Clubber
Closure, Cloture
Cockpit, Pockpit
Collect, Collate
Colonel, Coroner
Compose, Compile
Conceit, Concept
Concert, Concord
Concoct, Confect
Condole, Console
Confess, Concede
Confirm, Confine
Consist, Consent
Contend, Contest
Contest, Conteck
Context, Pandect
Contort, Distort
Contort, Misform
Control, Conduct
Contund, Contuse
Convene, Convoke
Copaiba, Copaiva
Cordial, Cardiac
Coroner, Crowner
Coroner, Colonel
Cotylae, Cotyles
Courier, Courser
Cramped, Crammed
Crankle, Crinkle, Wrinkle, Crunkle
Creased, Pressed
Created, Erected
Crimine, Crimini
Crisped, Creased

Crosier, Crozier
Crouper, Crupper
Crumple, Crunkle
Crypton, Krypton
Current, Torrent
Currier, Furrier
Custard, Costard
Cuvette, Cunette
Cyanate, Cyanite, Kyanite
Cyprian, Cypriot
Damosel, Damozel
Darling, Dilling
Daunder, Saunter
Dawning, Morning
Decamps, Levants
Decline, Recline
Degrade, Deprave
Delapse, Relapse
Deleble, Delible
Depress, Repress
Deprive, Reprive
Deposit, Reposit
Descant, Discant
Destine, Appoint
Destiny, Destine
Diarial, Diarian
Diarchy, Dyarchy
Diffuse, Suffuse
Dilator, Dilater
Discuss, Dispute
Dislike, Mislike
Dispone, Dispose
Distort, Misform, Disform
Divided, Divvied
Dogskin, Pigskin, Hogskin, Kipskin
Dogtrot, Foxtrot, Jogtrot
Dominus, Dominie
Donnerd, Donnert
Dracina, Dracine
Dribble, Trickle
Drizzle, Dribble
Dropped, Drooped
Droukit, Drookit
Drudged, Trudged
Drugget, Droguet, Drabbet
Dunfish, Sunfish, Dogfish
Dunnock, Pinnock
Dustman, Dustpan
Ebriose, Ebrious
Elastic, Plastic
Elusive, Evasive
Elytrum, Elytron
Embower, Imbower
Embrown, Imbrown
Emongst, Amongst
Empanel, Impanel
Emulate, Imitate
Enclose, Inclose
Endiron, Andiron
Endorse, Indorse
Endless, Express
Engross, Ingross
Engrain, Ingrain
Enlarge, Enhance
Enquire, Inquire
Ensnare, Insnare, Ensnarl

Enthral, Inthral
Entrant, Intrant
Entrust, Intrust
Entwine, Entwist
Entwist, Intwist
Epicism, Epicist
Erected, Created
Erector, Erecter
Estrich, Ostrich
Excheat, Escheat
Exclude, Extrude
Extract, Extreat
Extrude, Intrude, Obtrude
Faience, Fayence
Fanatic, Lunatic
Farther, Further
Fasting, Banting
Fatling, Catling
Felloes, Fellies
Fending, Fencing
Feodary, Feudary
Filacer, Filazer
Filbert, Filberd
Finnock, Finnack
Fitchet, Fitchew
Flacket, Flasket
Flashes, Glances
Flitted, Flirted, Fleeted
Flitter, Flicker, Flacker
Fluster, Bluster
Flutter, Flitter
Flutter, Fluster
Foliage, Foggage
Foolery, Feppery
Foxtrot, Dogtrot, Jogtrot
Foundry, Laundry
Fragile, Brittle
Francis, Frances
Frumple, Wrickle
Furbish, Furnish, Burnish
Furrier, Currier
Further, Farther
Gabbart, Gabbard
Gabelle, Gabeler
Gallant, Valiant
Galleon Galliot
Garland, Girlond
Garment, Raiment
Garnish, Furbish
Gateway, Pathway
Geogony, Geology
Gesture, Posture
Ghostly, Ghastly
Gittern (see Cithern)
Glances, Flashes
Glitter, Glisten, Glister
Globus, Globose
Gorilla, Zorille, Zorilla, Zorrino
Grandad, Grandma, Grandpa, Grandam
Grasped, Trapped
Griffin, Griffon
Grubble, Grabble
Grumous, Grumose
Guanaco, Huanaco
Gunboat, Bumboat, Tugboat
Hackler, Heckler

Haddock, Paddock
Hagweed, Ragweed
Halacha, Halakah
Halibut, Holibut
Hallion, Hallian, Hallyon
Halyard, Lanyard, Laniard
Handbag, Sandbag
Harlock, Hardock, Burdock
Harmful, Hurtful
Harries, Harrows
Hassock, Cassock
Hatrack, Hatrail
Haulage, Hallage
Herring, Herling, Merling
Hoggish, Piggish
Hogskin, Pigskin, Dogskin, Kipskin
Hommack, Hummock, Hammock
Honesty, Modesty
Hopbine, Hopbind
Huanaco, Guanaco
Humming, Bumming
Hundred, Cantred
Hurried, Hurtled
Hustler, Bustler, Justler, Rustler
Iceland, Ireland
Ignoble, Unnoble
Illicit, Illegal
Imbower, Embower
Imitate, Emulate
Immures, Impales
Impeach, Appeach
Impress, Imprese, Impresa
Include, Inclose, Enclose
Indorse, Endorse
Inflame, Inflate
Ingrain, Engrain
Ingross, Engross
Inquest, Inquiry
Inquire, Enquire
Install, Instate
Intrude, Obtrude, Extrude
Intrust, Entrust
Intwist, Entwist
Italian, Idalian
Jackdaw, Jacamar
Janitor, Monitor
Jannock, Bannock
Jealous, Zealous
Jemidar, Jamadar
Joggles, Jostles
Jogtrot, Dogtrot, Foxtrot
Joukery, Jookery
Juggins, Muggins
Kacodyl, Cacodyl
Kebbock, Kebbuck
Keramic, Ceramic
Ketchup, Catchup
Kettles, Ketches
Khutbah, Khotbah
Kipskin, Pigskin, Hogskin, Dogskin
Kirtles, Mantles

Knacker, Knocker
Kneecap, Kneepan
Knitted, Knotted
Knuckle, Truckle
Krypton, Crypton
Kumquat, Cumquat
Kyanite, Cyanite
Lameter, Lamiter, Lamiger
Lamprey, Pampern
Laniard, Lanyard, Halyard
Largest, Longest
Laundry, Foundry
Leaders, Readers
Lectern, Lettern
Leopard, Libbard
Levants, Decamps
Licence, License
Liquefy, Liquate
Lockram, Buckram
Lorimer, Loriner
Luggage, Baggage
Lunatic, Fanatic
Mandola, Mandora
Mandrel, Mandril
Manikin, Manakin
Manilla, Manilio, Manille
Mantles, Kirtles
Mantles, Mantlet
Mashlim, Mashlin, Mashlum
Maximum, Minimum
Merling, Herling, Herring
Message, Missive
Messiah, Messias
Million, Billion
Minever, Miniver
Minibus, Omnibus
Misform, Distort, Disform
Mislike, Dislike
Missive, Missile
Modesty, Honesty
Mollusk, Mollusc
Monarch, Nomarch, Toparch, Navarch
Monitor, Janitor
Morning, Dawning
Moulwee, Moulvie
Muddied, Muddled
Muffins, Biffins
Muggins, Juggins
Mugwort, Madwort
Mullion, Munnion
Murexes, Murices
Mystery, Secrecy
Nargile, Nargili
Navarch (see Monarch)
Negress, Negroes
Nervure, Nervule
Nomarch (see Monarch)
Nostrum, Rostrum
Nourish, Noursle, Nourice
Noxious, Nocuous
Noysome, Noisome
Oatcake, Pancake, Carcake
Obtrude, Intrude, Extrude
Octoped, Octopod
Octopod, Octopus
Odaller, Udaller

Omnibus, Minibus
Onshore, Inshore
Ostrich, Estrich
Outgoes, Outdoes
Outlive, Survive
Padding, Wadding
Paddock, Haddock
Paddock, Puddock
Pahlavi, Pehlevi
Painter, Printer, Pointer
Palaver, Palabra
Pandect, Context
Pandoor, Pandour
Pandore, Pandura, Bandore
Parotid, Parotis
Parsnip, Parsnep
Pasquin, Pasquil
Passion, Passive
Pathway, Gateway
Pauline, Paulina
Peacher, Teacher
Peevish, Pettish
Pendant, Pendent, Pending
Penguin, Pinguin
Pennant, Pendant
Pennate, Pinnate
Pergola, Pergula
Perhaps, Percase
Pervert, Distort
Piebald, Pyebald
Piffins, Biffins
Piggish, Hoggish
Pigskin, Kipskin
Pinfold, Penfold
Pinnock, Dunnock
Plaster, Blister
Pleases, Blesses
Plouter, Plotter
Plumber, Plummer
Plumous, Plumose
Plumule, Plumula
Pockpit, Cockpit
Pollaxe, Poleaxe
Pollock, Pollack
Postage, Portage, Pontage
Posting, Putting
Posture, Gesture
Pranced, Branked, Pranked
Preface, Prelude
Prejink, Perjink
Prelate, Primate
Premise, Premiss
Pressed, Creased
Pribble, Prabble
Pricket, Brocket
Printer, Painter, Pointer
Prithee, Prythee
Procure, Produce
Produce, Product
Promise, Proviso
Propose, Purpose, Purport
Provand, Provend
Pumpkin, Pumpion
Putting, Posting
Ragweed, Hagweed
Raiment, Garment
Rampart, Rampire
Rampick, Rampike
Rampion, Campion

Ranches, Ranchos
Ratchel, Ratchil
Ratline, Ratling
Ratteen, Satteen
Raymond, Raymund
Readers, Leaders
Recline, Decline
Rebound, Redound, Resound
Refiner, Refuser
Relapse, Delapse
Relieve, Release
Relievo, Rilievo
Relives, Revives, Regives, Revires
Reposit, Deposit
Reproof, Reprief
Request, Bequest
Require, Requere
Reserve, Silence
Retrace, Retract
Retreat, Retrate, Retract
Rhizome, Rhizoma
Roinish, Roynish
Rollock, Rullock, Rowlock
Ronchil, Ronquil
Rosalia, Rosalie
Rostrum, Nostrum
Rowboat, Towboat, Gunboat, Tugboat, Bumboat
Rulable, Regible
Rustler, Hustler, Bustler
Salient, Saliant, Saltant
Sambhar, Sambhur
Sandbox, Bandbox
Sandbag, Handbag
Sardine, Sargina
Sardine, Herring, Shadine
Satisfy, Satiate
Satteen, Ratteen
Saunter, Daunder
Scabble, Scapple
Scaddle, Skaddle
Scallop, Scollop
Scalpel, Scalper
Scatter, Swatter, Spatter
Sceptic, Skeptic
Scissel, Scissil
Scooper, Scorper
Scraggy, Scranky
Scranny, Scrawny
Screech, Scritch, Scraigh, Scraich, Spraich
Scrunch, Scranch
Scuppet, Scoppet
Scuttle, Scuddle, Skuttle, Scutter
Seating, Setting
Section, Lection
Serbian, Servian
Seriema, Cariama
Shackle, Shangle
Shanker, Chancre
Sharply, Shrilly
Sheriff, Shereef
Shippon, Shippen
Shyster, Shifter
Sienite, Syenite
Silence, Reserve
Similar, Similes

Sinopia, Sinopis
Sirloin, Surloin
Sirname, Surname
Sisters, Fosters
Sistine, Sixtine
Skeptic, Sceptic
Skuttle, Scuttle
Slashed, Slapped
Slobber, Slabber
Slyness, Sliness
Smuggle, Snuggle
Sniffle, Snuffle
Snipped, Snicked
Snirtle, Snortle
Soaring, Surging
Soldier, Soldado
Sonatas, Sonnets
Sonnite, Sunnite
Spacial, Spatial
Sparkle, Spangle
Sparrow, Swallow
Spinach, Spinage
Spirket, Sperket
Spousal, Sponsal
Spraich (see Screech)
Spulzie, Spulyie
Sputter, Stutter
Squabby, Squaddy
Squeeze, Squelch
Stagger, Swagger
Stamina, Stamens
Stammer, Sputter, Stutter
Staniel, Stanyel, Stannel
Started, Stirred
Stature, Statute
Stemple, Stempel
Stifled, Stilled
Stopper, Stopple
Storage, Stowage
Studies, Studios
Subadar, Subedar
Subduce, Subduct
Success, Succeed
Succory, Chicory
Suffuse, Diffuse
Survive, Outlive
Survive, Subsist
Sutlery, Butlery
Swallow, Sparrow
Swatter, Spatter, Scatter
Swimmer, Skimmer
Swollen, Swelled
Talcose, Talcous
Taliput, Taliput, Talipat
Tamilic, Tamulic
Tampion, Tompion
Tannage, Tanning
Tatters, Banters
Teacher, Peacher
Terrier, Tarrier, Harrier
Testify, Certify
Thither, Thether
Timpani, Timbals
Timpani, Timpano, Tympano
Titling, Titlark
Toparch (see Monarch)
Torrent, Current
Tortive, Tortile, Torsive
Towboat (see Rowboat)
Tramper, Tranter

Trapped, Grasped
Treadle, Treddle
Trickle, Dribble, Trinkle
Triduum, Triduan
Trindle, Trundle
Tripped, Trapped
Trivial, Fragile
Truckle, Knuckle
Trudged, Drudged
Tuatara, Tuatera
Tugboat, Gunboat, Bumboat
Tuilyie, Tuilzie
Tumbrel, Tumbril
Twofold, Twifold
Udaller, Odaller
Uncivil, Incivil
Unnoble, Ignoble
Valiant, Gallant
Variate, Variant
Vedette, Vidette
Vicious, Vitious
Villain, Villein
Violent, Fervent
Voivode, Vaivode, Vayvode, Waiwode, Waywode, Woiwode
Wadding, Padding
Waftage, Wafture
Waiwode, Waywode, Woiwode, Voivode, Vaivode, Vayvode
Wareful, Careful
Waxwing, Waxbill
Wearied, Worried, Harried
Weasand, Weazand
Webster, Wabster
Welsher, Welcher
Whaisle, Whaizle
Whemmle, Whommle, Whomble, Whummle
Whiffer, Whiffet
Whisper, Whimper
Whommle, Whomble, Whemmle, Whummle
Windock, Winnock
Wishful, Wistful
Wolfish, Wolvish
Woorali, Woorara, Wourali
Wrangle, Brangle
Wrinkle, Crinkle, Frumple
Yorling, Yolding
Younger, Younker
Zaptieh, Zabtieh
Zarebas, Zerebas
Zealous, Jealous
Zincali, Zingaro, Zingano
Zingari, Zingane,
Zithern (see Cithern)
Zoogeny, Zoogony
Zoolite, Zoolith
Zoology Zootaxy
Zorrino, Zorilla, Zorille, Gorilla

8 Letters or More

Abruption, Abreption
Accepted, Received
Accourage, Encourage

Adherence, Inherence, Inherency
Adherent, Inherent
Adjutant, Adjuvant
Aerodrome, Aerophone, Aeroplane
Alcaydes, Alcaides
Altercation, Alternation
Altitude, Attitude
Appendant, Attendant
Apricots, Apricock, Abricock
Ascribed, Assigned
Assurance, Insurance
Astrology, Astronomy
Attitude, Altitude
Attentive, Attending
Automobile, Locomobile
Bakhshish, Backshish, Baksheesh
Baneberry, Blaeberry
Bandoleer, Bandolier, Bandelier
Bannerol, Banderol
Banister, Baluster
Barbacan, Barbican
Baritone, Barytone
Barranca, Barranco
Batholite, Batholith
Benedict, Benedick
Bergamot, Burgamot
Bittacle, Binnacle
Bizcacha, Viscacha
Boarding, Hoarding
Bolshevik, Menshevik
Bookworm, Hookworm
Bountree, Bourtree
Bridegroom, Bridesmaid
Brothers, Brethren
Buccaneer, Buccanier
Budapest, Bukarest, Bucarest
Bullytree, Bolletric, Bulletrie
Burganet, Burgonet
Cabriole, Capriole
Cacholot, Cachalot
Calendar, Kalendar
Camisade, Camisado
Cannikin, Pannikin
Cariacou, Carjacou
Carriage, Carriole
Cauliflower, Colliflower
Celestine, Celestite
Centinel, Sentinel
Cephalic, Kephalic
Cevadilla, Cebadilla, Sabadilla
Chancellory, Chancellery
Checklaton, Shecklaton
Chincapin, Chinkapin
Chipmunk, Chipmuck
Chloride, Chlorate
Chlorodyne, Chloroform
Chrysalis, Chrysalid
Cingalese, Sinhalese
Cogitate, Meditate
Coistril, Coystrel, Coystril
Composer, Compiler
Confines, Confuses
Confiture, Comfiture

Conserve, Preserve
Contribute, Constitute
Cornelian, Carnelian
Costmary, Rosemary
Coverlet, Coverlid
Crawfish, Crayfish
Creosote, Creasote
Custodian, Custodier
Dandriff, Dandruff
Deadwind, Headwind
December, November
Delusive, Illusive
Dempster, Deemster
Depository, Repository
Depraved, Degraded
Describe, Descrive
Despatch, Dispatch
Destitute, Discharge
Detention, Retention
Devonport, Davenport
Diablery, Witchery
Difficult, Difficile
Dignitaries, Dignitarial
Dinarchy, Monarchy, Toparchy, Nomarchy, Navarchy
Disgrace, Disgrade
Dispense, Dispence
Distemper, Destemper
Distrust, Mistrust
Doomsday, Domesday
Draghound, Staghound
Drummock, Drammock
Dungeree, Dungaree
Education, Erudition
Embrangle, Imbrangle
Embroglio, Imbroglio
Encircle, Engirdle
Enclosed, Enclaved
Encourage, Accourage
Engouled, Engoulee
Engroove, Ingroove
Enhearse, Inhearse
Enswathe, Inswathe
Entrench, Intrench
Entrusted, Intrusted
Enveigle, Inveigle
Enwreathe, Inwreathe
Epicedial, Epicedian
Erection, Erecting
Escalade, Escalado
Escapade, Escapado
Excelled, Exceeded
Exception, Exemption
Explanation, Explication
Exterior, Interior
External, Internal
Fascisti, Fascists, Fascismo
Filipino, Filipina
Fillibeg, Philibeg
Flapjack, Slapjack
Flitting, Fleeting, Floating
Forcemeat, Mincemeat
Forecast, Foretell
Fortalices, Fortilages, Fortresses
Freckles, Speckles
Fruticose, Fruticous
Galleass, Galliass
Gambison, Gambeson

Garefowl, Gairfowl
Gargoyle, Gurgoyle
Garrison, Garnison
Gasalier, Gaselier
Gasometer, Manometer
Gerfalcon, Gyrfalcon
Gilravage, Galravage
Gimcrack, Jimcrack
Gingerale, Gingerade
Greesing, Gressing
Greywacke, Graywacke
Guaranty, Warranty
Hankered, Hungered
Headwind, Deadwind
Hebridean, Hebridian
Hedgehog, Hedgepig
Hoarding, Boarding
Hoarhound, Horehound
Hookworm, Bookworm
Horrible (see Terrible)
Hymeneal, Hymenean
Idolater, Zoolater
Idolatry, Zoolatry
Illusive, Delusive
Imbecile, Innocent
Imbrangle, Embrangle
Incitement, Inducement
Indicate, Intimate
Infantile, Infantine
Ingroove, Engroove
Inhearse, Enhearse
Inherent, Adherent
Inherence, Inherency,
  Adherence
Inofficial, Unofficial
Insanable, Incurable
Insurance, Assurance
Inswathe, Enswathe
Interfere, Intervene,
  Intercede
Interior, Exterior
Inverted, Reverted
Isabelle, Isabella
Ironwork, Ironware
Jimcrack, Gimcrack
Kalendar, Calendar
Kangaroo, Wanderoo,
  Wallaroo
Kautikoy, Canticoy
Kentledge, Kintledge
Kephalic, Cephalic
Laniferous, Lanigerous
Lichgate, Lychgate
Liniment, Linament,
  Ointment
Locomobile, Automobile
Linotype, Monotype
Locality, Vicinity,
  Vicinage
Loyalist, Royalist
Luncheon, Nuncheon
Lustrine, Lustring
Mackerel, Pickerel
Mahlstick, Maulstick
Mahomedan, Mahometan
Makebait, Makebate
Malarial, Malarian
Manducate, Masticate
Manifold, Multiple
Manometer, Gasometer
Manyplies, Maniplies,
  Monyplies

Marquetry, Parquetry
Massicot, Masticot
Mastered, Mustered
Maternal, Paternal,
  Parental
Measurable, Mensurable
Meditate, Cogitate
Menshevick, Bolshevick
Metacism, Mytacism
Metazoan, Metazoic
Millipede, Millepede
Mincemeat, Forcemeat
Mistletoe, Misseltoe
Mistrust, Distrust
Monarchy, Dinarchy,
  Toparchy, Nomarchy,
  Navarchy
Mongoose, Mungoose
Monotype, Linotype
Moorfowl, Moorcock
Murrhine, Myrrhine
Muscatel, Muscadel
Narration, Narrative
Naseberry, Neesberry
Nazarite, Nazirite
Neurotic, Neurosis
Nomarchy (see Dinarchy)
November, December
Ointment, Liniment,
  Linament
Oleander, Oleaster
Oscillate, Vacillate
Oughtness, Rightness
Overdone, Overgone
Pachalic, Pashalic
Paludine, Paludose
Pannikin, Cannikin
Parquetry, Marquetry
Parrakeet, Parroquet
Password, Passport
Patchouli, Patchouly
Patchbox (see Watchbox)
Patentee, Patenter,
  Patentor
Paternal, Maternal,
  Parental
Patricide, Matricide
Philibeg, Fillibeg
Pickapack, Pickaback
Pickerel, Mackerel
Plateaux, Plateaus
Pleasant, Pleasing
Plummery, Plumbery
Polliwig, Pollywig
Porpoise, Tortoise,
  Porpesse
Portfory, Portuary
Portoise, Portlast
Potshard, Potshare,
  Potsherd
Practice, Practise
Preserve, Conserve
Pretense, Pretence
Promoted, Prompted
Prosperity, Prosperous
Provider, Provedor,
  Provisor
Prunello, Prunella
Pruinose, Pruinous
Rebelled, Revolted
Received, Accepted
Reclusion, Seclusion

Redshank, Redstart
Reenforce, Reinforce
Renegade, Renegado,
  Renegate, Runagate
Retention, Detention
Repelled, Revolted
Repository, Depository
Reversed, Reverted
Reverted, Inverted
Rightness, Oughtness
Rosemary, Costmary
Royalist, Loyalist
Sabadilla, Cebadilla,
  Cevadilla
Sabeline, Zibeline
Sackless, Saikless
Safeguard, Saveguard
Sanhedrin, Sanhedrim
Sandiver, Sandever
Sangraal, Sangreal
Sapodilla, Zapotilla
Sarsenet, Sarcenet
Scallawag, Scallywag
Scarmage, Scarmoge
Sciatheric, Sciotheric
Scowther, Scouther
Scraffle, Scramble
Scribble, Scrabble
Scrimmage, Scrummage
Scuddick, Scuttock
Scuttled, Scurried
Sebestan, Sebesten
Seclusion, Reclusion
Seignior, Seigneur
Sentinel, Centinel
Seraphim, Teraphim
Serenade, Serenata
Shealing, Sheeling,
  Shieling
Shearing, Shedding
Shecklaton, Checklaton
Shillalah, Shilleiah
Shilling, Skilling
Shintiyan, Shintigan
Sinhalese, Cingalese
Siscowet, Siskiwit,
  Siskowet
Slapjack, Flapjack
Slippery, Sliddery,
  Slithery
Slipshod, Slipslop
Snowball, Snowfall
Sobranje, Sobranye
Soldiers, Soldiery
Soochong, Souchong,
  Pouchong
Soothsay, Southsay
Spadille, Spadilio
Sparling, Spirling,
  Spurling
Speckles, Freckles
Speldrin, Speldron
Sportive, Sporting
Sprackle, Sprachle
Sprattle, Scramble
Sprinkle, Strinkle
Squeaker, Squealer
Staghound, Draghound
Stagirite, Stagyrite
Stallion, Stellion
Stornello, Stornelli
Straggler, Struggler

Strictly, Straitly [gate
Strigous, Strigose, Stri-
Struggle, Sprangle
Submerge, Submerse
Sunflower, Safflower
Swastika, Svastika
Swingletree, Whiffletree,
  Whippletree
Sycamore, Sycamine
Sympathy, Symphony
Tamarind, Tamarisk
Tarantula, Tarentula
Tarlatan, Tarletan
Taximeter, Taxameter
Teachable, Tractable
Telephone, Telephote
Tendentious,   Tenden-
  cious
Teraphim, Seraphim
Terrible, Horrible,
  Terrific, Horrific
Terribly, Horribly,
  Horridly
Threnode, Threnody
Tirrivee, Tirrivie
Toparchy (see Dinarchy)
Tortoise, Porpoise,
  Porpesse
Translate, Transmute

Transmute, Transform
Transparent, Translucent
Trappean, Trappous
Trousers, Trowsers,
  Trossers
Turkoman, Turcoman
Unofficial, Inofficial
Vacillate, Oscillate
Valhalla, Walhalla
Valkyrian, Walkyrian
Varicose, Varicous
Vartabed, Vartabet
Ventriloquial, Ventrilo-
  quous
Verdigris, Verdegris
Vicinity, Vicinage,
  Locality
Viscacha, Bizcacha
Vitality, Virility
Waistband,   Waistbelt,
  Wristband
Walhalla, Valhalla
Walkyrian, Valkyrian
Wallaroo, Wanderoo,
  Kangaroo
Warranty, Guaranty
Watchbox, Patchbox,
  Matchbox

Watermole, Watervole
Wasegoose, Wayzgoose
Welladay, Wellaway
Whiniard, Whinyard
Whiffletree, Whippletree,
  Swingletree
Whiskyjack, Whiskyjohn
Whinstone, Whetstone
Whinstone, Whunstone
Whinstone, Whunstane
Wifehood, Wivehood
Witchery, Diablery
Withershins, Widdershins
Wolverene, Wolverine
Wrinkled, Wrizzled
Xylonite, Zylonite
Yearling, Yeanling
Yeldring, Yeldrock, Yold-
  ring
Youthhead, Youthhood
Zapotilla, Sapodilla
Zemindary,   Zamindari,
  Zemindari
Zibeline, Sabeline
Zoolater, Idolator
Zoolatry, Idolatry
Zumbooruk, Zamboorak
Zylonite, Xylonite

————————✳————————

ANIMALS, REPTILIA

2 Letters

Ai
Ky
Ox

3 Letters

Ape
Asp
Ass
Bat
Bay
Boa
Bok
Cat
Cob
Cow
Cub
Cur
Dam
Doe
Dog
Eft
Elk
Ewe
Fox
Gib
Gnu
Hog
Keb
Kid
Kit
Kob
Kye
Leo
Nag
Nix
Pig
Pom
Pug
Pup
Ram
Rat
Roe
Rug
Sai
Seg
Sow
Sug
Tag
Tat
Teg
Tod
Tup
Uta
Wat
Yak

4 Letters

Agua
Apis
Axis
Barb
Bawd
Bear
Boar
Boma
Buck
Bull
Cade
Calf
Cavy
Chow
Colt
Cony
Coon
Dauw
Deer
Dieb
Dood
Douc
Emys
Evet
Eyra
Fawn
Foal
Frog
Gate
Gaur
Gilt
Goat
Gyal
Hack
Hare
Hart
Hind
Hogg
Hyen
Ibex
Jack
Jade
Joey
Koba
Lama
Lamb
Lion
Lynx
Mare
Mink
Minx
Moco
Mohr
Moke
Mole
Mops
Mule
Musk
Naga
Naig
Naja
Neat
Newt
Once
Oryx
Owre
Oxen
Paca
Paco
Pala
Pard
Peba
Pica
Pony
Puma
Puss
Quey
Rach
Rack
Rana
Rane
Roan
Ruek
Rusa
Saki
Salp
Seal
Seps
Shot
Skug
Skye
Sore
Stag
Stot
Tahr
Thar
Tike
Toby
Tyke
Toad
Unau
Urus
Urva
Vari
Vole
Want
Wolf
Worm
Zati
Zebu
Zobo

5 Letters

Aboma
Addax
Adder
Agama
Agnus
Alant
Anura
Ariel
Aries
Asker
Aspic
Beast
Bever
Bidet
Biped
Bison
Bitch
Brach
Brawn
Brock
Bruin
Bugle
Burro
Camel
Caple
Capul
Cavey
Cebus
Civet
Coati
Cobra
Colly
Coney
Coypu
Crock
Cuddy
Daman
Dhole
Dicky
Dingo
Dipus
Draco
Drake
Drill
Dsomo
Dwarf
Eland
Elaps
Equus
Fauna
Felid
Felis
Ferae
Filly
Fitch
Fossa
Gayal
Gazel
Gecko
Genet
Gibbe
Goral
Grice
Grise
Helix
Hinny
Hobby
Horse
Hound
Husky
Hydra
Hyena
Hyrax
Izard
Jocko
Kaama
Kevel
Koala
Kokob
Krait
Kyloe
Lemur
Llama
Loris
Magar
Magot
Manis
Meles
Micky
Mooly
Moose
Morse
Mouse
Muley
Mully
Myall
Nagor
Nanny
Neddy
Nixie
Nyula
Okapi
Orang
Otary
Otter
Ounce
Panda
Pekan
Phoca
Pongo
Poulp
Puppy
Pussy
Rasse
Ratch
Ratel
Rhino
Roger
Sable
Saiga
Sajou
Salpa
Sasin
Scrub
Sheep
Shier
Shoat
Shock
Simia
Skink
Skunk
Snail
Snake
Sobol
Spitz
Staig
Steed
Steer
Stirk
Stoat
Stote
Swine
Tabby
Tacky
Talpa
Taxel
Thous
Tiger
Tucan
Urial
Urson
Viper
Vison
Vixen
Waler
Whelp
Yapok
Zebra
Zerda
Zhobo
Zibet
Zizel
Zoril
Zorra
Zorro

6 Letters

Agouta
Agouti
Albino
Aliped
Alpaca
Angola
Angora
Anolis
Anoura
Argali
Aspick
Ayeaye
Baboon
Bandog
Barbet
Basset
Bawsin
Bayard
Beagle
Beaver
Beeves
Boomer
Borzoi
Bow-wow
Bronco
Brumby
Buglet
Bunyip
Cabrie
Cabrit
Caiman
Canuck
Castor
Cayman
Cayuse
Cervus
Chacma
Chetah
Coaita
Cocker
Collie
Corsac
Cosset
Cougar
Coyote
Cuddie
Curtal
Cuscus
Dandie
Desman
Dickey
Dikdik
Dipsas
Dobbin
Dodman
Donkey
Dragon
Dugong
Duiker
Durham
Duyker

			7 and 8 Letters		
Dzeren	Limmer	Russel		Giraffe	Mungoose
Dzeron	Lionel	Sagoin		Gorilla	Musquash
Ellops	Lionet	Saguin	Aardvark	Guanaco	Mustang
Ermine	Lizard	Sambar	Aardwolf	Guereza	Nasalis
Estray	Malkin	Samboo	Acalepha	Hanuman	Narwhal
Farrow	Margay	Sambur	Acouchy	Harrier	Nylghau
Fennec	Marmot	Sarlac	Actinia	Hatteria	Olifant
Ferret	Marten	Sarlak	Anaconda	Hexapod	Oliphant
Fummel	Mawkin	Semele	Annelid	Hobbler	Oppossum
Funnel	Messin	Serval	Annelida	Hoggerel	Panther
Galago	Monkey	Shough	Antelope	Huanaco	Peccary
Garial	Mugger	Simpai	Arvicola	Hydromys	Pegasus
Garran	Musang	Sleuth	Assinego	Hystrix	Polecat
Gavial	Musmon	Sorrel	Aurocks	Jackass	Polypode
Gennet	Mutton	Spalax	Babirusa	Jararaka	Potoroo
Geomys	Mouton	Sponge	Bathorse	Kangaroo	Pottoroo
Gibbon	Narwal	Steare	Baudrons	Keitloa	Pygopus
Gibcat	Natrix	Styrax	Behemoth	Kitling	Raccoon
Gimmer	Nilgai	Taguan	Blesbok	Kolinsky	Reindeer
Ginnet	Nutria	Talbot	Bubalis	Lagomys	Roodebok
Gopher	Ocelot	Tangum	Buffalo	Leopard	Sabella
Hackee	Onager	Tanrec	Capucine	Leveret	Sarigue
Harier	Ovibos	Tapeti	Capybara	Libbard	Septaria
Heifer	Padnag	Tarpan	Caribou	Lobworm	Sondeli
Hircus	Pallah	Teetee	Chamois	Lugworm	Spaniel
Hogget	Palolo	Teledu	Cheetah	Macaque	Squirrel
Howler	Panter	Tenrec	Chelonia	Madoqua	Steinbok
Hyaena	Poodle	Theave	Cheviot	Manatee	Tamarin
Iguana	Porker	Tomcat	Chipmuck	Mangabey	Terrier
Inyala	Porket	Towser	Chipmunk	Mandrill	Tuatera
Jackal	Pyrame	Tupaia	Colobus	Mandrine	Twinter
Jaguar	Python	Turtle	Dolphin	Markhor	Vicugna
Jennet	Rabbit	Uakari	Echidna	Marmose	Wallaby
Jerboa	Racker	Urchin	Elephant	Marmoset	Wallaroo
Jibber	Racoon	Vermin	Entozoa	Mastiff	Wanderoo
Jiboya	Ramcat	Vervet	Entozoon	Mastodon	Warragal
Jowler	Ranger	Vicuna	Ermelin	Mongoose	Warrigal
Jumart	Ratter	Walrus	Fitchet	Monocle	Whinnook
Jument	Reebok	Weasel	Fitchew	Monster	Whippet
Kalong	Regina	Wombat	Foumart	Mormopes	Xenurus
Kennel	Rhebok	Wow-wow	Gazelle	Moschus	Zamouse
Kitten	Rhesus	Wretch	Gemsbok	Moufflon	Zonurus
Koodoo	Riggle	Yapock		Mongoose	
Kraken	Rodent				

BIRDS AND INSECTS

2 Letters	Fum	Ree	Chat	Fowl	Kaka
Ka	Hen	Roc	Cleg	Frit	Kell
	Jay	Rok	Cock	Fung	Kite
3 Letters	Kae	Ruc	Coot	Gnat	Kiwi
	Kea	Tit	Crax	Gowk	Knot
Ant	Keb	Tui	Crow	Grig	Lark
Auk	Mew		Dodo	Grub	Loom
Bee	Moa	4 Letters	Dorr	Guan	Loon
Cob	Nye		Dove	Gull	Lory
Daw	Owl	Alca	Duck	Hawk	Maws
Dop	Pea	Anas	Emeu	Hern	Mina
Dor	Pen	Aves	Erne	Huia	Moth
Emu	Pie	Barb	Eyas	Ibis	Muff
Fly	Poe	Boud	Flea	Kagu	Myna

Nyas	Drone	Scoby	Cigala	Mistle	Tingis
Pavo	Dunne	Scops	Coccus	Mopoke	Tipula
Pern	Eagle	Scout	Cochin	Musket	Tomtit
Pica	Egret	Scull	Condor	Muslin	Topaza
Piet	Eider	Scray	Corbie	Mygale	Toucan
Pupa	Ember	Senex	Coucal	Nandoo	Towhee
Rail	Emmet	Serin	Crabro	Nestor	Tremex
Rhea	Finch	Sesia	Cuckoo	Nicker	Tringa
Rixy	Frank	Shama	Culver	Nitter	Tsetse
Ront	Gamma	Sitta	Curlew	Nympha	Turaco
Rook	Gaunt	Skart	Cushat	Oriole	Turbit
Rout	Geese	Snipe	Cygnet	Osprey	Turdus
Ruff	Glede	Soree	Darter	Oxbird	Turkey
Rukh	Goose	Spink	Dayfly	Pajock	Turnus
Runt	Goura	Spiza	Dipper	Parrot	Turtle
Rype	Grebe	Sprug	Diurna	Parson	Weevil
Shag	Gygis	Squab	Dogbee	Pastor	Whidah
Skua	Harpy	Stork	Dorado	Peaher	Whydah
Smee	Heron	Strix	Dryfly	Pecker	Wigeon
Sora	Hobby	Tarin	Ducker	Peewit	Willet
Sore	Homer	Terek	Dunlin	Pernis	Windle
Swan	Jager	Tiddy	Eaglet	Petrel	Witwal
Taha	Junco	Tinea	Earwig	Phasma	Xenops
Teal	Larus	Twite	Eirack	Pigeon	Yaffie
Tern	Liver	Urile	Epeira	Plover	Yowley
Tick	Louse	Urubu	Eyrant	Pouter	Yucker
Uria	Loxia	Veery	Falcon	Powter	Zabrus
Wasp	Macaw	Velia	Fulmar	Puffin	Ziczac
Wavy	Madge	Vespa	Gadfly	Pullet	
Wren	Merle	Vireo	Gaggle	Queest	**7 and 8**
Xema	Midge	Wader	Gambet	Quelea	**Letters**
Yaup	Mormo	Wavey	Gander	Rallus	
Yite	Musca	Whaup	Gannet	Redcap	Acarina
Yoit	Nandu	Whilk	Garrot	Rhesus	Acridian
Yunx	Noddy	Yacou	Gentoo	Rhyssa	Aigrette
Zimb	Ortyx	Zebub	Godwit	Roberd	Alcatras
	Osite		Grakle	Rotche	Allerion
5 Letters	Oubit		Grouse	Ruddoc	Apteryx
	Ousel	**6 Letters**	Hacket	Rumkin	Arachnid
Agami	Ouzel		Hagden	Rutela	Arapunga
Amsel	Owlet	Acarus	Haglet	Sapyga	Ascaris
Amzel	Oxfly	Alcedo	Hareld	Scamel	Assapan
Anana	Pewet	Alcyon	Hoazin	Scarab	Bittern
Annet	Pewit	Ananas	Hoopoe	Scaury	Bockelet
Aphid	Picus	Ancona	Hoopoo	Sciara	Buceros
Aphis	Piper	Anhima	Hopdog	Scobby	Buphaga
Ardea	Pipit	Antlia	Hopfly	Scolia	Burrhel
Argus	Poult	Argala	Hornet	Scoter	Buzzard
Biddy	Pulex	Ashfly	Houdan	Scurff	Capuchin
Booby	Pulse	Avocet	Howlet	Seabar	Cockatoo
Borer	Purre	Avoset	Jabiru	Seamew	Colibri
Bowet	Quail	Bantam	Jacana	Sepsis	Cotinga
Brant	Queen	Barbet	Jerkin	Serica	Dabchick
Brent	Quink	Beetle	Jigger	Shrike	Darcall
Brize	Radge	Bembex	Kakapo	Sicsac	Darcock
Bucco	Ralph	Blatta	Keelie	Silpha	Didapper
Capon	Raven	Bombyx	Kiddow	Simbil	Dipchick
Chick	Razor	Bonxie	Lanner	Simorg	Dobcherel
Chuck	Reeve	Botfly	Leipoa	Simurg	Dorking
Cimex	Rissa	Bowess	Linnet	Siskin	Dotterel
Clock	Robin	Brahma	Lintie	Slater	Duckbill
Colin	Rodge	Breese	Locust	Smeath	Ephemera
Comma	Rudge	Breeze	Maggot	Snabby	Estrich
Covey	Sagra	Bugong	Magpie	Sowbug	Estridge
Crake	Saker	Bulbul	Mantis	Spider	Finnikin
Crane	Salda	Cagmag	Martin	Strich	Flamingo
Culex	Sally	Canary	Mayfly	Strick	Gadwall
Curre	Samia	Chafer	Merlin	Tampan	Gerfalcon
Daker	Sasia	Chewet	Merula	Teaser	Gorcock
Dicky	Scarf	Chinch	Midget	Termes	Gorcrow
Diver	Scart	Chough	Miller	Thecla	Gosling
Drake	Scaup	Cicada	Missel	Thrush	Grackle
		Cicala			

Greylag	Jedcock	Mosquito	Pochard	Shoebill	Tinnock
Grosbeak	Judcock	Muggent	Poultry	Sparrow	Titlark
Guacharo	Kamichi	Notornis	Quetzal	Spathura	Titling
Gyrfalcon	Kestrel	Ortolan	Raptores	Spizella	Titmouse
Halcyon	Killdee	Ostrich	Redwing	Stannel	Umbrette
Hamburg	Kingbird	Partrick	Remigia	Starling	Vanessa
Hickwall	Kiroumbo	Partridge	Ringdove	Strepera	Wagtail
Hickway	Lannaret	Pandion	Rittock	Swallow	Wasebill
Hoatzin	Lapwing	Peacock	Ruddock	Tabanus	Whetile
Hornbill	Laverock	Pelican	Sacodes	Tanager	Widgeon
Hornowl	Mallard	Penguin	Salamis	Tarrock	Whimbrel
Impeyan	Marshhen	Pinguin	Saperda	Termite	Wrannock
Jackdaw	Marshtit	Pinnock	Sassorol	Throstle	Wrybill
Jacamar	Martinet	Pintail	Seacrow	Tinamou	Wryneck
Jacksaw	Megapode		Shanghai		

FISH

3 Letters

	Dare	Banny	Powan	Bowfin	Meager
Bar	Dart	Barmy	Prawn	Braize	Mennad
Bib	Dorn	Basse	Prill	Buckie	Minnow
Cod	Dory	Beryx	Quarl	Burbot	Morgay
Dab	Esox	Binny	Roach	Caplin	Mullet
Eel	Faap	Bleak	Roker	Carvel	Muscle
Fox	Gedd	Bleck	Ruffe	Cheven	Mussel
Fry	Goby	Boops	Saith	Chiton	Myaria
Gam	Grig	Bream	Sarda	Clupea	Myxine
Gar	Hake	Brill	Scate	Cockle	Nerite
Hag	Huck	Bulla	Scrod	Colmey	Ostrea
Hux	Huso	Capon	Sepia	Comber	Oyster
Ide	Jack	Chama	Shark	Conger	Partan
Lob	Kelt	Chank	Skate	Conner	Pecten
Mya	Ling	Charr	Smelt	Cowrie	Pholas
Orc	Lomp	Conch	Smolt	Cuttle	Plaice
Par	Loon	Cowry	Smout	Dentex	Plaise
Pod	Luce	Cuddy	Smowt	Derbio	Pollan
Ray	Opah	Doree	Snook	Diodon	Porgie
Sar	Orca	Dorse	Solen	Dipnoi	Poulpe
Tai	Parr	Elver	Sprag	Doggar	Rangia
Tau	Pike	Fleck	Sprat	Dorado	Redeye
	Pink	Fusus	Sprod	Elleck	Remora
4 Letters	Pope	Gadus	Squid	Ellops	Retzia
	Pout	Gibel	Tench	Finner	Rhinae
Amia	Quid	Hacot	Togue	Fumado	Rimula
Apod	Quin	Haked	Torsk	Gadean	Robalo
Arca	Rudd	Julis	Trout	Gadoid	Roccus
Bass	Ruff	Loach	Tunny	Gambet	Romero
Blay	Sapo	Loche	Turbo	Gardon	Ruffin
Bley	Scad	Lythe	Twait	Garvie	Sabalo
Bret	Scup	Maray	Umber	Germon	Sadina
Brit	Shad	Moray	Whale	Gilpin	Salmon
Burt	Sole	Mugil	Whelk	Ginkin	Samlet
Butt	Tope	Muray		Goramy	Sander
Carp	Zant	Murex	**6 Letters**	Hackle	Sardel
Chad		Murry		Haddie	Sargus
Char	**5 Letters**	Mysis	Allice	Grilse	Sarsia
Chub		Myxon	Anabas	Ivigar	Sauger
Clam	Ablen	Pearl	Angler	Jerkin	Saurus
Clio	Ablet	Perch	Barbel	Limpet	Saynay
Crab	Acera	Pogge	Beluga	Loligo	Scarus
Cusk	Allis	Porgy	Blenny	Maigre	Seabat
Dace	Angel	Poulp	Bonito	Maties	Semele

Sephen	Zander	Barnacle	Grampus	Mackerel	Scallop
Shanny	Zingel	Bloater	Grundel	Merling	Selache
Sierra		Bluefish	Gurnard	Mormyrus	Shadine
Soosoo	**7 and 8**	Bluepoll	Gwyniad	Pandora	Siskiwit
Tarpon	**Letters**	Calamory	Haddock	Pickerel	Smerlin
Tarpum		Crayfish	Hagfish	Pilchard	Sockeye
Tautog	Albacore	Crawfish	Halibut	Pipefish	Spirula
Tomcod	Albicore	Decapod	Herling	Pomfret	Spurling
Trigla	Alewife	Dogfish	Herring	Quinnat	Sterlct
Trygon	Ammo-	Flounder	Homelyn	Redfish	Stingray
Turbot	dyte	Frasling	Jentling	Ripsack	Sturgeon
Turtle	Anableps	Garfish	Keeling	Ronchil	Torpedo
Wapper	Anchovy	Gilthead	Lampern	Ronquil	Umbrine
Weever	Asterias	Gladius	Lamprey	Sardelle	Whiting
	Atherine	Goldney	Lobster	Sardine	Whitling

TREES, PLANTS, FRUITS AND FLOWERS

2 Letters	Yew	Diss	Lote	Sunn	Arbor
Ti	Zea	Dock	Mate	Tang	Areca
		Dohl	Mint	Tare	Areng
3 Letters	**4 Letters**	Doob	Moly	Taro	Arnot
Ash	Acer	Doum	Moss	Teak	Arnut
Asp	Ague	Dura	Musk	Teff	Arrow
Awn	Akee	Ejoo	Nabk	Teil	Aspen
Ban	Alfa	Eugh	Nard	Tine	Aspic
Bay	Aloe	Faam	Neep	Toon	Aster
Ben	Anil	Faba	Okra	Tree	Avens
Big	Arum	Fern	Palm	Tule	Bacca
Box	Avel	Flag	Pear	Tuna	Basil
Bur	Balm	Flax	Pepo	Tutu	Beech
Cos	Bean	Gage	Pine	Ulex	Berry
Elm	Bear	Gale	Pink	Upas	Betel
Fig	Beet	Gall	Plum	Vine	Bhang
Fir	Bene	Gaub	Poon	Wald	Birch
Fog	Bent	Gean	Ragi	Weed	Bixin
Haw	Bere	Geum	Rape	Weld	Blite
Hay	Bigg	Gill	Rata	Whin	Bloom
Hep	Bind	Gool	Reed	Woad	Bract
Hip	Blea	Goss	Rhea	Wort	Brake
Hop	Boom	Gram	Rhus		Brank
Ivy	Burr	Gule	Rice	**5 Letters**	Briar
Jak	Bury	Hemp	Rise		Brier
Kex	Cane	Herb	Rone	Abaca	Briza
Koa	Cive	Holm	Rose	Abele	Broom
Lis	Coca	Hurt	Rush	Abhal	Buchu
Nep	Coco	Ilex	Ruta	Abies	Bugle
Oak	Cola	Iris	Sadr	Acini	Bussu
Oat	Cole	Ixia	Sage	Acorn	Cacao
Oca	Coir	Jack	Sago	Agave	Calix
Pea	Cone	Kail	Seed	Ajuga	Calla
Rib	Corm	Kaki	Sego	Alder	Canna
Rie	Corn	Kale	Shea	Algae	Caper
Rue	Culm	Kali	Sida	Algum	Carex
Rye	Dali	Kans	Sium	Almug	Carob
Sal	Dari	Kola	Skeg	Ament	Cedar
Seg	Date	Leek	Slae	Anana	Chard
Tea	Dhak	Lily	Sloe	Anise	Chich
Tod	Dika	Lime	Sola	Anona	Chili
Yam	Dill	Ling	Soma	Apium	Chive
		Loco	Sorb	Apple	Cibol

Cicer	Maqui	Spike	Borage	Fennel	Nostoc
Clary	Mebos	Spink	Borago	Fescue	Nuphar
Clove	Medic	Stipa	Botree	Filago	Nutmeg
Cocoa	Melic	Stock	Braird	Fimble	Oidium
Coker	Merry	Sumac	Bryony	Fiorin	Orache
Colza	Morel	Swede	Burnet	Frutex	Orange
Copra	Moril	Tansy	Burrel	Fucoid	Orchid
Couch	Morus	Taxus	Busket	Fungal	Orchil
Cress	Mudar	Thorn	Byssus	Fungia	Orchis
Cubeb	Mulga	Thyme	Cactus	Fungus	Origan
Cumin	Naiad	Tingi	Camass	Funkia	Orrice
Cutch	Navew	Tryma	Camata	Fustet	Oxalis
Cycad	Noops	Tuart	Carapa	Fustic	Paeony
Daisy	Nopal	Tucum	Cardol	Galban	Paigle
Daroo	Ofbit	Tulip	Carica	Galega	Peanut
Doorn	Olive	Typha	Carrot	Galium	Peplis
Doura	Onion	Ulmus	Cashew	Garlic	Pepper
Draba	Orach	Uredo	Cassia	Garrya	Phasel
Drupe	Orris	Urena	Catnip	Gatten	Phleum
Dryad	Orval	Vetch	Caudex	Gervao	Pickle
Dulse	Oryza	Vinca	Cedrat	Gervas	Pippin
Durio	Oshac	Viola	Celery	Gingko	Pisang
Durra	Osier	Vitex	Cereus	Ginkgo	Platan
Dwale	Oxeye	Vitis	Cherry	Gomuti	Pomelo
Dwarf	Oxlip	Wahoo	Chilli	Gomuto	Poplar
Elder	Padma	Whort	Cicely	Groser	Potato
Eleot	Pagle	Wicky	Cicuta	Harmel	Privet
Enemy	Palas	Yacca	Cissus	Hedera	Protea
Erica	Palay	Yapon	Cistus	Hypnum	Pteris
Ficus	Panax	Yucca	Citron	Hyssop	Punica
Fitch	Pansy	Yulan	Clover	Iberis	Quinoa
Flora	Papaw	Yupon	Cockle	Jambul	Quitch
Fouat	Peach	Zamia	Codlin	Jarrah	Radish
Fouet	Pecan		Coffee	Jujube	Raffia
Frail	Peony	**6 Letters**	Coleus	Kalmia	Raggie
Fucus	Phlox		Collet	Kiekie	Raisin
Furze	Picea	Acacia	Collum	Laurel	Ramoon
Glary	Pipal	Acacio	Conium	Lentil	Raphia
Glaux	Pipul	Acajou	Conyza	Lichen	Ratany
Gobbo	Plane	Aceric	Coonty	Linden	Rattan
Goold	Poppy	Agaric	Corcle	Locust	Redbud
Gorse	Prune	Alisma	Cornel	Lolium	Reseda
Gourd	Pyrus	Almond	Corozo	Loquat	Restio
Gowan	Ramee	Alpine	Corymb	Lupine	Retama
Grape	Ramie	Alpist	Cowage	Luzula	Rhexia
Grass	Ratan	Alsike	Crocus	Macaco	Riccia
Guaco	Rheum	Amomum	Croton	Madder	Rivina
Guava	Rhyne	Ananas	Cummin	Mallee	Rochea
Halfa	Ribes	Annual	Curari	Mallow	Roddin
Hazel	Rivet	Antiar	Curcas	Mammee	Rosula
Heath	Roble	Arbute	Cuscus	Manioc	Royena
Hedge	Rogue	Arnica	Dahlia	Marram	Ruppia
Henna	Rohan	Arundo	Daphne	Marron	Ruscus
Holly	Rubia	Azalea	Darnel	Marrow	Russet
Iulus	Rubus	Bajree	Datura	Matico	Sabine
Julus	Rumex	Balsam	Daucus	Mazard	Sagina
Jambu	Runch	Bamboo	Delice	Medick	Sallow
Kecks	Sabal	Banana	Deluce	Medlar	Salvia
Larch	Savin	Banian	Deodar	Milium	Samara
Ledum	Savoy	Banyan	Desmid	Mimosa	Samyda
Lemon	Salix	Baobab	Dhurra	Mugget	Sapium
Liana	Sauch	Barley	Dodder	Mullen	Savine
Loofa	Saugh	Batata	Drupel	Muscat	Scilla
Lotos	Savin	Bellis	Durian	Myrica	Secale
Lotus	Scrab	Bennet	Eddoes	Myrtle	Seggan
Luffa	Scrub	Bennut	Egriot	Myrtus	Senega
Lupin	Sedge	Betony	Elaeis	Nardoo	Sesame
Madar	Sedum	Biffin	Endive	Nardus	Sesban
Madia	Shrub	Bizard	Eringo	Nargil	Seseli
Mahwa	Solah	Blewit	Eryngo	Nerine	Shalot
Mango	Solar	Bocage	Exogen	Nerium	Sheoak
Maple	Sorus	Boodle	Farina	Nettle	Sicyos

Silene	Allspice	Cassava	Guaiacum	Milfoil	Ruellia
Simson	Amaranth	Castanea	Hagberry	Milkwort	Saffron
Sindoc	Amaracus	Catalpa	Hagweed	Moonseed	Salsilla
Sintoc	Amellus	Catchfly	Hairbell	Mulberry	Salvinia
Smilax	Amorpha	Champac	Hardock	Mullein	Sambucus
Sorrel	Amphigen	Champak	Hartwort	Muscoid	Samolus
Souari	Anacord	Charlock	Hautboy	Mustard	Samphire
Spurge	Anemone	Chervil	Hawthorn	Nelumbo	Sanicle
Squill	Angelica	Chicory	Heather	Nigella	Sapindus
Styrax	Apricot	Cinnamon	Hemlock	Oleaster	Sapucaia
Sumach	Arbutus	Clematis	Henbane	Oleander	Sarcodes
Sundew	Arenaria	Cocculus	Hepatica	Onoclea	Sargasso
Tampoe	Asphodel	Comfrey	Higtaper	Orchanet	Scallion
Teasel	Auricola	Coquilla	Hockherb	Palmetto	Scandix
Teazel	Auricula	Corylus	Hornbeam	Palmyra	Scirpus
Tewart	Banksia	Corypha	Hornnut	Panicum	Seggrom
Tinguy	Barberry	Costard	Hottonia	Papyrus	Shamrock
Titree	Bergamot	Costmary	Hyacinth	Pareira	Shallot
Tomato	Bilberry	Cowslip	Isoetes	Parella	Shittah
Tooart	Blawort	Cowtree	Jasmine	Parsley	Skirret
Torula	Blossom	Cucumber	Jonquil	Paxiuba	Solanum
Trigyn	Boletus	Currant	Juniper	Pentzia	Solidago
Tupelo	Bourtree	Cypress	Kitefoot	Phormium	Sophora
	Boxelder	Daffodil	Knapweed	Pillwort	Starwort
7 and 8 Letters	Boxthorn	Deutzia	Lavender	Pimenta	Sultana
	Boxtree	Digynia	Larkspur	Pimento	Sweetbay
	Bracken	Dittany	Lentisk	Pipetree	Sweetpea
Abdalavi	Bramble	Dogwood	Lettuce	Plantain	Sycamore
Abelmosk	Brassica	Drosera	Lobelia	Platane	Sycamine
Abricock	Bromelia	Epiphyte	Lungwort	Plumcot	Syringa
Absinth	Buckbean	Esparto	Lupulus	Pollard	Tamarack
Acantha	Burdock	Filberd	Lychnis	Polyanth	Thapsia
Acanthus	Burreed	Filbert	Madrona	Primrose	Touraco
Achenium	Cabbage	Fragaria	Madwort	Primula	Turnsole
Aconite	Calabash	Fuchsia	Magnolia	Prunella	Valerian
Acrogen	Calamint	Galangal	Mahogony	Purslain	Verbena
Adiantum	Caltrops	Gardenia	Mallows	Purslane	Vervain
Agrimony	Calumba	Genipap	Malmsey	Quassia	Wallaba
Ailanto	Camellia	Gentian	Mandrake	Ragweed	Waratah
Alconet	Camomile	Geranium	Mangrove	Ragwort	Wistaria
Alkanet	Campana	Ginseng	Margosa	Rampion	Woodruff
Alfalfa	Campion	Girasole	Marigold	Rhubarb	Wychelm
Allgood	Canella	Gloxinia	Marjoram	Robinia	Xylopia
Allheal	Caraway	Godetia	Marybud	Roccella	Yeldring
Allhenna	Carline	Gromwell	Mezereon	Rosemary	Yeldrock

COINS AND MONEY

3 Letters		4 Letters			5 Letters
	Mag		Gelt	Merk	
Bit	Mil	Anna	Gold	Mill	Angel
Bob	Pie	Bill	Gowd	Mite	Arles
Ecu	Rap	Buck	Jane	Obol	Asper
Hog	Red	Cash	Joey	Para	Batta
Joe	Ree	Cent	Kite	Peso	Bodle
Lac	Rei	Chip	Lakh	Pice	Brass
Lat	Sen	Dime	Lira	Quid	Crore
Leu	Sou	Doit	Lire	Real	Crown
Lit	Sol	Dust	Maik	Rial	Dinar
Lev	Tin	Geld	Mail	Rino	Ducat
	Zuz		Mark	Ryal	

		6 Letters		**7 and 8 Letters**	
Eagle	Penny		Kopeck		Johannes
Franc	Plack		Kronen		Kreutzer
Groat	Pound	Bawbee	Kroner	Ambrosin	Maravedi
Krone	Bezant	Bezant	Mouton	Angelot	Milreis
Liard	Rhino	Byzant	Nickel	Assignat	Moidore
Litas	Ruble	Copeck	Peseta	Cardecu	Napoleon
Livre	Royal	Copper	Rouble	Carolus	Pfennig
Louis	Rupee	Couter	Silver	Centime	Piastre
Mopus	Scudi	Decume	Specie	Crusado	Picayune
Noble	Scudo	Denier	Stiver	Ducatoon	Pistole
Obang	Shahi	Dollar	Tanner	Farthing	Quadrano
Obdus	Shand	Escudo	Tester	Groschen	Scuddick
Ochre	Toman	Florin	Turner	Guilder	Scuttock
Lucre	Wheel	Guinea	Turney	Joannes	Shilling
Pence	Zloty	Gulden	Wampum		Skilling
		Kobang			

INSTRUMENTS (MUSICAL, ETC.), TOOLS

2 Letters	Gong	Blade	Sitar	Pliers	Calipers
	Grin	Bolas	Steel	Plyers	Castanet
Ax	Harp	Brace	Swage	Proker	Cithara
	Hawk	Brake	Tabor	Racket	Cithern
3 Letters	Heck	Bugle	Thole	Rammer	Clarinet
	Helm	Burin	Waddy	Ramrod	Clarion
Act	Horn	Crowd	Wecht	Rebeck	Clavecin
Adz	Iron	Dowel		Ripper	Coulter
Awl	Jack	Elsin	**6 Letters**	Ripsaw	Cremona
Axe	Kent	Flail		Rypeck	Curette
Dog	Lure	Fleam	Beetle	Sancho	Curtleax
Fan	Lute	Flisk	Bobbin	Scythe	Euphonon
Gad	Lyre	Flute	Bodkin	Tabour	Fagotto
Gue	Main	Gadge	Bolter	Tackle	Fidicula
Hoe	Mall	Gavel	Bougie	Tingle	Fistula
Kit	Oboe	Gauge	Brayer	Tymbal	Flutina
Nib	Pick	Groin	Buckle	Violin	Gimblet
Nut	Pike	Gyves	Cornet	Zither	Gittern
Oat	Prog	Jemmy	Creese		Grubber
Pen	Pump	Jimmy	Crease	**7 and 8 Letters**	Hackbut
Pin	Rack	Jenny	Cymbal		Halberd
Rod	Rake	Knife	Deckle	Ammeter	Hatchet
Saw	Rote	Knout	Douche	Andiron	Hatchel
Sax	Sang	Lance	Fiddle	Aneroid	Hautboy
Zax	Tool	Level	Fuller	Anelace	Hookpin
Zel	Trap	Lever	Gimlet	Angelot	Horologe
	Tuba	Lewis	Grater	Arbalest	Hornpipe
4 Letters	Tube	Madge	Graver	Arbalist	Javelin
	Viol	Naker	Guitar	Arblast	Lancegay
Adze	Weel	Organ	Hackle	Bagpipe	Linchpin
Bill	Whip	Paddy	Hammer	Balance	Machete
Brad	Worm	Pedal	Hangar	Bandore	Mandril
Brog	Zarf	Pilum	Harrow	Barnacle	Matchet
Card	Zurf	Plane	Heckle	Bassoon	Mattock
Celt		Poker	Kibbie	Bayonet	Melodeon
Club	**5 Letters**	Quirt	Launce	Bellows	Musette
Dirk		Ratch	Mallet	Billhook	Obelisk
Drum	Auger	Rebec	Mashie	Binocle	Ocarina
File	Banjo	Rocta	Needle	Bipennis	Odometer
Fork	Belty	Romal	Octant	Blunger	Pandore
Gage	Bevel	Shawm	Pestle		
Goad					

Panpipe	Pickaxe	Sackbut	Scuppet	Timbrel	Tweezers
Phorminx	Piffero	Samisen	Serpette	Timpano	Udometer
Pianette	Pincers	Saxhorn	Sistrum	Trammel	Violone
Pianino	Pinchers	Scalpel	Sordono	Triblet	Virginal
Pianola	Plunger	Scalper	Spatula	Trilabe	Woldhorn
Pibroch	Puncheon	Scoppet	Strocal	Trumpet	Zuffolo
Piccolo	Quintole	Scorper	Theorbo		

WEIGHTS AND MEASURES

2 Letters	4 Letters	Mile	Ardeb	Toise	Skekel
	Tun	Nail	Bekah	Verst	Windle
As	Weg	Pack	Candy	Yojan	Yojana
Em		Page	Carat		
En	4 Letters	Palm	Catty	6 Letters	7 and 8
Li	Acre	Peck	Chain		Letters
	Bath	Pica	Coomb	Arroba	
3 Letters	Bent	Pole	Ephah	Bandle	Acherset
	Boll	Pood	Homer	Barrel	Centner
Are	Comb	Ream	Liang	Bundle	Chaldron
Cab	Cord	Riyo	Liter	Bushel	Chalder
Cor	Coss	Role	Litre	Carrat	Deciare
Ell	Cran	Rood	Livre	Chopin	Decigram
Erg	Demy	Rope	Maneh	Cantar	Drachma
Fou	Dram	Rotl	Maund	Fathom	Footrule
Hin	Epha	Seah	Meter	Firkin	Furlong
Ion	Foot	Shot	Metre	Firlot	Hectare
Kat	Gill	Tael	Minim	Fother	Mutchkin
Lay	Gram	Tare	Ounce	Gallon	Parasang
Log	Hand	Tola	Pearl	Gramme	Puncheon
Mil	Hank	Tsun	Perch	League	Quadrant
Ohm	Hide	Vara	Pound	Minute	Quarter
Oke	Knot	Yard	Quire	Modins	Quintal
Pud	Hour		Quart	Moment	Stadium
Rio	Inch	5 Letters	Score	Mouton	Tonnage
Tod	Last		Stone	Octavo	Tunnage
Ton	Link	Anker	Todde	Second	

DRINKS AND FOOD (THINGS EDIBLE)

3 Letters	Cod	Hog	Peg	4 Letters	Bran
	Cud	Ice	Pie		Bree
Ale	Dop	Jam	Rob	Azym	Broo
Ama	Egg	Mum	Rug	Bean	Bull
Ava	Fry	Nip	Rum	Beef	Cake
Bap	Gin	Nog	Sop	Beer	Cate
Bub	Gum	Nut	Soy	Beet	Chop
Bun	Ham	Oat	Tea	Bisk	Crab

	5 Letters		6 Letters		7 and 8 Letters	
Duck	Apple	Puree	Comfit	Turtle		Gherkin
Duff	Azyme	Salmi	Confit	Wherry		Hardbake
Eats	Bacon	Scone	Congee	Waffle		Haricot
Eggs	Bingo	Shrab	Conjee	Walnut		Hoecake
Fare	Bread	Shrub	Damper	Whisky		Hog-
Farl	Bohea	Sirop	Entree			manay
Food	Brawn	Sirup	Gateau	7 and 8		Hollands
Fool	Brose	Spice	Geneva	Letters		Hydromel
Fowl	Broth	Steak	Grouse			Kedgeree
Hare	Bumbo	Sugar	Haggis	Aleberry		Ketchup
Hash	Cabob	Swats	Hominy	Alegill		Kruller
Hock	Candy	Sweet	Junket	Alicant		Lollipop
Kava	Caper	Syrup	Kipper	Alicante		Lozenge
Lamb	Cates	Toddy	Liquid	Ambrosia		Licorice
Lard	Chops	Tripe	Liquor	Banbury		Macaroon
Loaf	Cider	Trout	Malaga	Bannock		Malmsey
Meal	Cocoa	Viand	Mutton	Biffins		Marsala
Meat	Cress	Wafer	Nacket	Biscuit		Mosclle
Mush	Curry	Water	Nocake	Bordeaux		Muscadel
Must	Cyder		Omelet	Brisket		Muscatel
Pate	Flour	6 Letters	Orange	Brocoli		Oatcake
Pear	Fruit	Alegar	Oxymel	Cabbage		Omelette
Port	Gorja	Almond	Panada	Carcake		Oporice
Pull	Gravy	Amrila	Parkin	Caromel		Pancake
Purl	Gruel	Arrack	Pastry	Catchup		Pikelet
Raki	Hogan	Banana	Perkin	Caviare		Pikelin
Roll	Honey	Beaune	Pickle	Chablis		Porridge
Rusk	Kandy	Bisque	Pilque	Charqui		Preserve
Sack	Lager	Bonbon	Plaise	Cheddar		Pudding
Sole	Lemon	Brandy	Potato	Chowder		Ratafia
Soup	Mango	Burgoo	Prawns	Chutnee		Rissole
Stew	Medoc	Bitter	Ragout	Confect		Sandwich
Suet	Melon	Butter	Rabbit	Conserve		Sausage
Tack	Morat	Caviar	Salmis	Cosaque		Saveloy
Tape	Negus	Celery	Salmon	Crowdie		Sillabub
Tart	Onion	Cherry	Sherry	Custard		Slapjack
Tent	Pasty	Coffee	Spirit	Drum-		Spinach
Tuck	Patty	Coudle	Squash	mock		Succade
Veal	Peach	Claret	Sunket	Dumpling		Tapioca
Whig	Perry	Cheese	Tipper	Eggflip		Tortilla
Wine	Punch	Chewet	Tipple	Flapjack		Whiskey
Wort		Coffee	Tomato	Fritter		Whitepot
			Turnip	Gauffre		

MATERIALS, FABRICS AND DRESS

3 Letters	4 Letters			5 Letters	
	Baft	Drab	Lawn	Suit	Atlas
Alb	Bead	Duck	Mask	Tayo	Baize
Bib	Belt	Fall	Mitt	Tete	Beige
Boa	Boot	Felt	Muff	Tile	Black
Bow	Buff	Garb	Mull	Tire	Busby
Cap	Busk	Gear	Pall	Toga	Camis
Fez	Call	Gown	Plug	Toge	Chaco
Hat	Capa	Haik	Poke	Veil	Claes
Mat	Cape	Harn	Pump	Vest	Cloak
Obi	Cask	Helm	Rail	Wear	Cloth
Rag	Caul	Hood	Robe	Weed	Clout
Rep	Clog	Hose	Ruff	Wrap	Crape
Rig	Coat	Hyke	Sack		Crash
Rug	Coif	Jean	Sari	5 Letters	Derby
Taj	Cope	Jump	Shag		Drill
Tog	Cowl	Kelt	Shoe	Acton	Ephod
Wig	Cuff	Kepi	Silk	Amice	Fanon
		Kilt	Sock	Apron	Frock
		Lace	Stud	Armet	Front

Gauze	Voile	Collar	Sandal	Chapeau	Necktie
Glove	Wigan	Corset	Shorts	Chasuble	Orarium
Habit		Cotton	Shroud	Chemise	Organdie
Jabot	**6 Letters**	Cravat	Sontag	Chopine	Orleans
Jadoo		Draper	Tabard	Corduroy	Pabouche
Jasey	Albert	Domett	Tippet	Corsage	Paduasoy
Jupon	Bangle	Domino	Turban	Costume	Pajamas
Khaki	Barret	Duffel	Ulster	Cothurn	Paletot
Linen	Barrow	Gaiter	Vellet	Cracowes	Pallium
Mitre	Basque	Garter	Velvet	Cretonne	Pantofle
Moire	Beaver	Galosh	Wimple	Dalmatic	Parasol
Pants	Biggin	Golosh	Wodmal	Damassin	Petasus
Perse	Blazer	Helmet		Drilling	Pinafore
Plume	Blouse	Jacket	**7 and 8**	Dungaree	Placket
Plush	Bodice	Jerkin	**Letters**	Epaulet	Poulaine
Print	Bonnet	Jersey		Fillibeg	Prunella
Pshaw	Bowler	Jubbah	Aillette	Fingroms	Puggree
Rabat	Breeks	Jumper	Apparel	Flannel	Puttees
Sabot	Brogue	Kimono	Armozeen	Foulard	Putties
Sagum	Brogan	Kirtle	Armozine	Galatea	Pyjamas
Satin	Brooch	Livery	Baboosh	Galoche	Rateen
Scarf	Brutus	Mantle	Baffetas	Gambroon	Ratteen
Scarp	Burrel	Manton	Balmoral	Gingham	Sarsenet
Serge	Buskin	Mantua	Bandana	Havelock	Sattara
Shako	Bustle	Melton	Bandeau	Himation	Slipper
Shawl	Caddis	Merino	Barracon	Jackonet	Soubise
Shift	Calash	Mitten	Bashlyk	Jamdari	Subucula
Shirt	Calico	Morion	Basinet	Jamewar	Surplice
Skirt	Calpac	Muslin	Benjamin	Lingerie	Tabaret
Slops	Camese	Napron	Bernouse	Lockram	Taffeta
Smock	Camise	Nebris	Biretta	Lustring	Taffety
Spats	Camiso	Patten	Blancard	Mantelet	Tallith
Talma	Camlet	Peruke	Blanket	Mantilla	Tarlatan
Tiara	Canvas	Poncho	Blucher	Moleskin	Tiffany
Tibet	Capote	Poplin	Boxcoat	Montero	Troosers
Toile	Casque	Pugree	Brodekin	Mouchoir	Trousers
Topee	Castor	Puttee	Buckram	Muffetee	Trowsers
Tunic	Casula	Puttie	Burnoose	Muffler	Tussore
Tweed	Chintz	Rochet	Camisole	Nainsook	Vareuse
Twill	Coatee	Rockel	Cassock	Nankeen	Vigonia
				Neckband	Woollen

VEHICLES

3 Letters	Pram	Cycle	Calash	Sleigh	Caravan
	Pulk	Float	Chaise	Surrey	Cariole
Bus	Shay	Ginny	Camion	Tandem	Caroche
Cab	Sled	Larry	Clatch	Telega	Carriage
Car	Taxi	Lorry	Dennet	Trosky	Clarence
Fly	Tram	Lurry	Dhooly	Troika	Cornwain
Gig	Trap	Motor	Doolie	Tumtum	Dhoolie
Rig	Tube	Pulka	Drosky	Waggon	Droshky
Van	Wain	Racer	Fiacre	Whisky	Flivver
		Sedan	Gharri		Hackery
4 Letters	**5 Letters**	Slipe	Gharry	**7 and 8**	Kibitka
		Sueky	Gocart	**Letters**	Norimon
Arab	Araba	Tonga	Jampan		Phaeton
Auto	Aroba	Train	Jigger	Autocar	Quadriga
Bier	Berth	Truck	Kafila	Barouche	Ricksha
Bike	Bogey	Wagon	Landau	Bicycle	Rickshaw
Buss	Bogie		Limber	Britzska	Tilbury
Carr	Brake	**6 Letters**	Litter	Brougham	Tumbrel
Cart	Buggy		Palkee	Cacolet	Tumbril
Chay	Coach	Barrow	Pulkha	Caisson	Vettura
Drag	Coupe	Berlin	Sledge	Caleche	Victoria
Dray					
Mail					

RECEPTACLES AND VESSELS

3 Letters

Ark
Bac
Bag
Bin
Box
Can
Cap
Cat
Cod
Cog
Cot
Cub
Cup
Dan
Dow
Fat
Hod
Hoy
Jar
Jug
Keg
Kid
Kit
Man
Mug
Net
Nog
Pan
Pen
Pig
Pix
Pod
Pot
Pyx
Sac
Tig
Tin
Tot
Tub
Tug
Tun
Urn
Vas
Vat

4 Letters

Back
Bail
Bark
Bath
Bing
Boat
Boil
Boll
Bowl

Brig
Bush
Buss
Butt
Caba
Cade
Cage
Case
Cask
Cist
Cock
Corb
Corf
Dhow
Dish
Etna
Etui
Ewer
Grab
Hask
Hulk
Jack
Junk
Kong
Keel
Keir
Kipe
Kist
Lamp
Leap
Mull
Oast
Olla
Olpe
Pail
Pink
Poke
Pram
Proa
Punt
Rack
Sack
Saic
Sail
Scow
Ship
Skep
Skip
Snow
Tank
Tass
Till
Tray
Trug
Vase
Vein
Vial
Yowl

5 Letters

Ampul
Ashet
Basin
Barge
Billy
Buist
Bulse
Bursa
Burse
Caddy
Canoe
Casco
Chest
Coble
Cogie
Cogue
Coper
Craft
Crare
Crate
Creel
Crewe
Crock
Cruet
Cruse
Cupel
Dandy
Dilli
Dilly
Dingy
Drake
Ferry
Flask
Glass
Hanap
Hutch
Joram
Jorum
Keeve
Ketch
Ladle
Laver
Liner
Lotah
Mound
Motto
Phial
Pinky
Plate
Pouch
Proam
Scoop
Scree
Scrip
Sharp
Shout

Sieve
Sirop
Skeel
Skiff
Sloop
Spoon
Stean
Steen
Stoop
Stoup
Tazza
Temse
Tinny
Trink
Whiff
Xebec
Zabra
Zebec

6 Letters

Argosy
Backet
Barque
Barrel
Basket
Bateau
Beaker
Beetle
Bicker
Billie
Bireme
Bottle
Bucket
Budget
Bunker
Caique
Carack
Carafe
Carboy
Carton
Casket
Caster
Ceroon
Chatty
Cobble
Coffer
Coffin
Coggie
Copper
Cotyla
Crayer
Cruset
Cutter
Dingey
Dipper
Dogger
Dolium
Flacon

Flagon
Galley
Girnet
Goblet
Hamper
Hooker
Hopper
Howker
Hydria
Kettle
Kibble
Kulpis
Launch
Locket
Lugger
Magnum
Marque
Noggin
Patera
Pelike
Pewter
Piggin
Pipkin
Posnet
Pottle
Quaigh
Randan
Retort
Riddle
Rummer
Runner
Sachel
Sachet
Sampan
Sandal
Sanpan
Saucer
Seroon
Serpet
Shovel
Siphon
Syphon
Tassie
Teacup
Teapot
Teaurn
Trowel
Tureen
Wallet
Wherry
Wisket

7 and 8 Letters

Abditory
Alembic
Almsbox
Amphora

Ampulla
Balloon
Bandbox
Barrico
Benitier
Bilander
Billyboy
Binnacle
Birlinn
Caldron
Cannikin
Canteen
Capsule
Caravel
Cauldron
Chaldron
Chalice
Cistern
Collier
Columba
Corvette
Costrel
Cresset
Crucible
Cruiser
Felucca
Flivver
Frigate
Gabbard
Galleass
Galleon
Galliot
Hogshead
Jeroboam
Knapsack
Lymphad
Padella
Pannier
Pannikin
Patamar
Patella
Pericarp
Pitcher
Platter
Polacca
Pontoon
Reticule
Sagathy
Satiere
Samovar
Satchel
Satchet
Schooner
Skippet
Solander
Steamer
Trinket
Whisket

PRONOUNS

2 Letters	3 Letters			5 Letters	6 Letters
As	Any	The	Ourn	Their	Either
Em	Hem	Who	Ours	These	Itself
He	Her	You	That	Thine	Myself
It	Him		Thee	Those	Theirs
Me	His	**4 Letters**	Them	Which	
My	Its	Both	They	Whose	
Us	One	Else	This	Whoso	
We	Our	Hern	Thou		
Ye	She	Hers	What		
		Mine	Whom		

EXCLAMATIONS AND INTERJECTIONS

2 Letters	3 Letters				
Ah	Aha	Out	Bosh	Whoa	Hallo
Ay	Ave	Pah	Chut	Yoho	Hello
Bo	Bah	Poh	Dear		Hillo
Ha	Boo	See	Easy	**5 Letters**	Holla
Hi	Fie	Tut	Egad	Alack	Hollo
Ho	Foh	Ugh	Euge	Avast	Hullo
Jo	Gad	Wow	Hail	Bedad	Marry
La	Hah		Hech	Begad	
Lo	Hem	**4 Letters**	Hist	Bravo	**6 Letters**
Oh	Hep	Ahem	Hush	Faugh	Avaunt
On	Hey	Ahoy	Phew	Gadso	Barley
	Hie	Alas	Pooh	Haith	Behold
	Hoa	Amen	Soho	Heigh	Holloa
	Hoy	Away	Tata	Hence	Parley
		Booh	Toho		
			Whew		

PREPOSITIONS

2 Letters			5 Letters		
At	Ere	Near	Abaft	Circa	Around
By	For	Next	About	Emong	Bating
In	Fro	Nigh	Above	Forth	Before
Of	Off	Onto	Adown	Intil	Behind
On	Out	Over	Afore	Round	Beside
Or	Per	Past	After	Since	Beyond
To		Post	Along	Under	Except
Up	**4 Letters**	Save	Among	Until	Inside
	Amid	Till	Anear		Saving
3 Letters	Baft	Unto	Anent		Toward
Ben	Down	Upon	Astir	**6 Letters**	Versus
But	From	With	Below	Aboard	Withal
	Into			Across	Within
				Amidst	

DO YOU KNOW THAT—

BOTH S.M. and H.M. are abbreviations for "His" or "Her Majesty" (abb).

F.R.S. and S.R.S. are both correct abbreviations for "Fellow of the Royal Society."

S.D. is the correct abbreviation for " Sends Greetings."

The abbreviation for Keeper of the Privy Seal is C.P.S.

Peapod, although a fairly common word, is missing from many dictionaries.

Both A.B. and B.A. are correct for " Bachelor of Arts " (abb.) and so are A.M. and M.A. for "Master of Arts " (abb.).

"Compare" is abbreviated C. P. or C. F.

O.D. and O.S. both stand for " Ordinary Seaman " (abb.).

A.C. and B.C. are both possible for "Before Christ " (abb.).

Bachelor of Surgery is abbreviated B.S., whilst Master of Surgery is C.M.

AU and OR = Gold;	AG = Silver;
CU = Copper;	FE = Iron;
ER = Erbium;	HG = Mercury;
MG = Magnesium;	NI = Nickel;
PT = Platinum;	SN = Tin;
ZN = Zinc.	

Doctor of Divinity (abb.) may be D.D. or D.T.

Num and Nos are both abbreviations of " Numbers."

E.G. and V.G. are abbreviations of "for example," but that Ex. means "Example."

The Signs of the Zodiac are: **Aries** (Ram); **Aquarius** (water-bearer); **Capricorn** (Goat); **Cancer** (Crab); **Gemini** (Twins); **Leo** (lion); **Libra** (balance); **Pisces** (Fishes); **Scorpio** (Scorpion); **Sagittarius** (Archer); **Taurus** (Bull); **Virgo** (Virgin).

WORDS WITH SIMILARITY OF MEANING

In the following pages will be found a number of words grouped together and which have some similarity of meaning.

These have been arranged in word size opposite a suggested clue (which is of necessity somewhat wide), and it must be emphasised that they are intended merely as pointers to possible solutions.

A definition in the dictionary of the clue word in your square may possibly suggest one of the clue words given here. Those suggested solutions which are of the required size can then be traced in your dictionary, when you can satisfy yourself whether or not they are apt answers to the clue you have to solve.

Compilers are continually introducing fine shades of meaning into the clues, so that it is imperative to reiterate that your dictionary must be consulted on every occasion.

ABSOLVE	Pardon, Acquit, Settle, Remove, Remedy, Verdict, Release
AVOW	Declare, Justify, Confess, Promise, Affirm, Ratify, Announce, Maintain
ASK	Seek, Pray, Prog, Look, Inquire, Request, Solicit, Invite, Appeal, Indite, Debate, Consider, Question, Converse
AID	Help, Loan, Subsidy, Support, Succour, Assist, Relief, Remedy
AIL	Afflict, Trouble, Disturb, Agitate, Annoy, Molest, Ill, Bad
AIM	Design, Direct, Intent, Effect, Result, Purpose, Purport
ABATE	Deduct, Lessen, Weaken, Reduce, Shrink, Contract, Diminish
ABUSE	Pervert, Violate, Corrupt, Deceive, Defile, Infect, Debase
ACUTE	Sly, Fly, Eager, Sharp, Acute, Biting, Severe, Argute, Astute, Shrill, Shrewd
AGREE	Accede, Assent, Concur, Settle, Determine, Harmonise, Consent, Concord
ABIDE	Stop, Stay, Linger, Endure, Remain, Suffer, Sustain, Undergo
ABILITY	Power, Skill, Master, Expert, Faculty, Strength, Capacity

ABRIDGE	Shorten, Curtail, Deprive, Lessen, Reduce, Modify, Change
ADMINISTER	Manage, Impose, Conduct, Execute, Adjust, Settle
ADVANCE	Promote, Propose, Improve, Increase, Enhance
AGITATE	Observe, Discuss, Examine, Consider, Argument, Ponder, Wonder
ALERT	Brisk, Sharp, Awake, Aware, Alert, Quick, Swift, Agile
ANNUL	Quash, Sweep, Disbar, Depose, Ignore, Cancel, Revoke, Repeal, Recant
ALLOCATE	Cite, Gift, Give, Name, Place, Allot, Refer, Parcel, Divide, Allege, Appoint, Transfer, Commit, Direct
ALLOW	Admit, Grant, Agree, Leave, Abate, Permit, Invest, Concur, Assert, Consent, Support
ARDENT	Polite, Intent, Fervid, Eident, Burning, Serious, Earnest, Zealous, Impetuous, Irritable
ARRAY	Fig, Rig, Dress, Order, Equip, Adorn, Class, Conduct, Arrange
APPLY	Ask, Write, Assign, Impute, Employ, Ascribe, Request
APPOINT	Grant, Equip, Devote, Settle, Assign, Bestow, Decree
APPAREL	Dress, Adorn, Guise (see Section Dress, Materials, etc.)
ARTICLE	Attack, Impose, Charge, Indict, Burden, Enjoin, Accuse, Clause, Command, Custody
ASCEND	Tower, Mount, Climb, Ascent, Raise, Hoise, Hoist
ARTFUL	Clever, Crafty, Cunning, Knowing, Skilful
ASSAY	Try, Pry, Strive, Strife, Effort, Attempt, Examine, Define, Affect
ASSUAGE	Ease, Calm, Help, Abate, Allay, Quiet, Settle, Soften, Remove, Lessen, Support, Redress, Release, Diminish, Mitigate
ASSURE	Secure, Insure, Ensure, Plight, Pledge
ATONE	Agree, Quiet, Allay, Reconcile, Harmonise
ATTACH	Bind, Band, Bond, Join, Fasten, Arrest, Adhere, Cohere, Inhere, Conjoin, Connect
ATTAIN	Get, Win, Gain, Earn, Obtain, Arrive, Procure, Acquire, Receive
ATTEND	Heed, Care, Notice, Remark, Civility, Courtesy, Escort, Direct
ATTEST	Witness, Testify, Certify, Protest, Declare, Avow, Aver
ATTIRE	(See Section Dress, Materials) Dress, Adorn, Array, Fig, Rig
AUSTERE	Sober, Harsh, Grave, Rough, Tough, Weighty, Serious
BAD	Faulty, Wicked, Imperfect, Defective, Blamable, Painful, Hurtful, Harmful, Incorrect, Imperfect
BAFFLE	Cheat, Check, Cover, Hoodwink, Bewilder, Disgrace, Disgrade
BAG	Nap, Mag, Sac, Sack, Pack, Steal, Seize, Pinch, Pouch, Swell
BAIT	Food, Fret, Lure, Worry, Harry, Tease, Annoy, Choke, Fatigue, Torment
BALE	Fire, Evil, Pyre, Parcel, Bundle, Misery, Injury, Misfortune, Affliction
BALK	Pass, Beam, Avoid, Evade, Evite, Check, Elude, Ridge, Ignore, Swerve, Refuse, Reject, Refute
BAND	Bond, Bind, Bend, Ruff, Gang, Ring, Pack, Belt, Link, Body, Slip, Troop, Group, Chain, Space, Confine, Company
BANK	Rank, Tier, Bench, Table, Ridge, Mound, Mount, Money, Stage
BANTER	Joke, Gest, Assail, Attack, Impose, Rag, Gag, Rig, Chaff, Rally
BASE	Bass, Mean, Vile, Foot, Root, Game, Deep, Grave, Lowly, Servile, Debased, Modest, Humble
BARB	Horse, Point, Sting, Beard, Shave, Hair, Down
BAY	Tree, Bark, Yelp, Yell, Space, Crown, Utter, Watch, Chase, Horse, Inlet, Recess, Laurel, Renown

BARK Tan, Yap, Ship, Yelp, Rive, Skin, Peel, Pell, Pill, Barge, Utter, Strip, Speak, Cough

BITE Cut, Eat, Nab, Nap, Nim, Nip, Rip, Rit, Pain, Tear, Rend, Hurt, Harm, Feed, Food, Catch, Seize, Sting, Cheat, Trick, Break, Wreck, Crush, Frush, Wound, Enter, Deceive, Defraud, Seizure, Corrode, Inflict, Affect, Pierce

BEAR Bere, Bigg, Wear, Bier, Carry, Admit, Press, Imply, Ursus, Endure, Afford, Relate, Suffer, Import, Animal, Demean, Manage, Behave, Support, Cherish, Produce, Sustain

BEAT Hit, Mix, Sound, Wound, Pulse, Pound, Rouse, Break, Throb, Place, Shape, Weary, Tired, Tread, Knock, Strike, Bruise, Thrash, Resort, Stroke, Conquer, Agitate, Pulsate

BEND Tie, Bow, Jut, Lean, Turn, Crook, Crank, Curve, Fasten, Subdue, Strain, Curved, Direct, Incline, Deflect

BLOT Spot, Blob, Blow, Blet, Mark, Rain, Sully, Taint, Fault, Stain, Patch, Defect, Efface, Darken, Reduce, Destroy, Expunge, Blemish, Disfigure, Discolour

BLACK Dim, Dye, Dark, Dull, Soil, Moil, Smut, Moor, Void, Soot, Dirt, Empty, Dusky, Negro, Dirty, Blank, Speck, Dress, Blind, Shade, Heavy, Colour, Vacant, Sombre, Gloomy, Sullen, Dismal, Misery, Cloudy, Wicked, Horrible, Terrible, Terrific, Dreadful, Mournful

BLINK Wink, Pink, Hint, Peer, Peep, Peek, Evade, Evite, Shirk, Avoid, Shine, Gleam, Spark, Glint, Glisk, Quiver, Quaver, Glance, Sparkle, Twinkle, Glimmer, Glimpse, Glitter, Glisten, Glister

BLOW Tap, Rap, Pat, Wap, Hit, Fan, Brag, Gale, Wind, Beat, Pant, Puff, Fuff, Ovum, Bloom, Knock, Drive, Taint, Shock, Sound, Spout, Spurt, Light, Boast, Breath, Flower, Spread, Report, Shatter, Inflate, Current, Blossom, Display, Calamity, Disaster

BODY Form, Mass, Bulk, Club, Gang, Ging, Lump, Trunk, Frame, Solid, Group, Shape, Stiff, Staff, Troop, Matter, Person, Number, Middle, Corpse, Ground

BRIGHT Brisk, Witty, Clear, Clean, Light, Sharp, Smart, Happy, Noble, Alive, Agile, Alert, Quick, Swift, Active, Nimble, Wimble, Clever, Shining, Glorious, Cheerful, Brightly, Sanguine, Unclouded

BREAK Tear, Rend, Rent, Rest, Ruin, Rift, Part, Tame, Drag, Open, Down, Frame, Burst, Force, Wreck, Crush, Train, Twist, Frush, Crock, Brock, Check, Utter, Pause, Breach, Brooch, Change, Appear, Weaken, Impair, Subdue, Lessen, Soften, Shatter, Sputter, Rupture, Destroy, Outrage, Violate, Dismiss, Cashier, Decline, Disable, Opening, Disperse, Suspense, Degrade, Collapse, Separate, Dissolve, Carriage, Interrupt, Intercept

BUTT But, End, Bunt, Push, Cask, Mark, Sole, Fish, Goal, Hide, Abut, Mound, Trunk, Stump, Limit

CALL Cap, Cry, Name, Hail, Cite, Lure, Cause, Shout, Summon, Appeal, Signal, Regard, Select, Reckon, Demand, Invoke, Appoint, Command, Summons, Address, Convoke, Impulse, Whistle, Occasion, Proclaim, Consider, Describe

CANT Tip, Kip, Dip, Sale, Vent, Keen, Toss, Sell, Jerk, Talk, Turn, Tilt, Angle, Lusty, Speak, Slang, Brisk, Sharp, Slant, Slope, Jargon, Active, Strong, Lively, Thrust, Incline, Auction, Dialect

CALM Balm, Ease, Easy, Eath, Meek, Stop, Lull, Quiet, Peace, Allay, Still, Sleep, Abate, Repose, Soothe, Placid, Serene, Smooth, Silent, Gentle, Peaceful, Sedative, Moderate, Tranquil

CAST Turn, Wind, Last, Look, Shed, Emit, Hurl, Draw, Drew, Mien, Make, Form, Drop, Warp, Throw, Threw, Mould, Fling, Flung, Allot, Sling, Slung, Shape, Stamp, Shade, Thing, Tinge, Drive, Motion, Reckon, Squint, Degree, Glance, Assign, Scheme, Chance, Manner, Colour, Direct, Assign, Condemn, Quality, Compute, Company, Venture, Contrive, Consider

CARRY Show, Wear, Bear, Tote, Gain, Lead, Draw, Have, Reach, Imply, Ferry, Convey, Import, Effect, Extend, Manage, Demean, Behave, Propel, Deport, Contain, Display, Conduct, Support, Transport, Enrapture

CATCH Nip, Nab, Nap, Gin, Cog, Hold, Song, Stop, Trip, Trap, Play, Seize, Cling, Check, Grasp, Clamp, Clasp, Cramp, Carry, Notch, Adhere, Cohere, Inhere, Entrap, Arrest, Snatch, Cleave, Attach, Fasten, Engage, Ensnare, Ensnarl, Seizure, Receive, Connect, Surprise, Entangle, Interrupt, Intercept

CAUSE Case, Sake, Fault, Excuse, Yield, Motive, Reason, Object, Affair, Matter, Produce, Product, Because, Subject, Dispute, Grounds

CHARGE	Lay, Put, Fix, Set, Tax, Bid, Fill, Load, Care, Duty, Rush, Cause, Order, Exact, Onset, Entry, Office, Enter, Price, Value, Burden, Enjoin, Powder, Exhort, Attack, Impose, Govern, Impute, Accuse, Deliver, Command, Custody, Entrust, Intrust, Control, Message, Obligation, Commission, Accusation
CHIP	Hew, Cut, Nag, Rag, Mag, Hag, Chop, Clip, Crop, Pare, Mock, Slip, Joke, Jest, Josh, Quid, Bore, Coin, Trim, Rail, Part, Wear, Break, Crack, Tease, Split, Piece, Slice, Chink, Smack, Detach, Deride, Banter, Impose, Ridicule, Derision, Fragment
CHECK	Stop, Stay, Stem, Mark, Term, Halt, Test, Ease, Place, Token, Order, Chide, Cloth, Repel, Refel, Pause, Rebel, Scold, Rebuke, Hinder, Hamper, Cheque, Rebuff, Ticket, Defeat, Refuse, Refute, Recuse, Control, Voucher, Pattern, Reproof, Reprove, Compare, Reverse, Repulse, Restrain, Stoppage
CHUCK	Tap, Pat, Rap, Hit, Blow, Game, Call, Toss, Hurl, Call, Jerk, Yerk, Pitch, Noise, Chick, Throw, Touch, Fling
CIRCLE	Arc, Orb, Ring, Move, Body, Rove, Room, Patch, Orbit, Range, Limit, Ambit, Girth, Period, Cycle, Class, Argue, Virole, Circus, Series, Number, Extent, Sphere, Enclose, Circuit, Compass, Surround, Encircle, Engirdle
CLASP	Join, Hold, Hook, Link, Catch, Joint, Hinge, Grasp, Cling, Pivot, Buckle, Brooch, Device, Fasten, Embrace, Receive
CLEAR	Pure, Mere, Bare, Neat, Trim, Free, Leap, Jump, Pass, Holy, Fine, Fair, Thin, Nice, Keen, Quite, Plain, Clean, Empty, Lucid, Vivid, Profit, Serene, Remove, Remble, Bright, Acquit, Settle, Wholly, Evident, Certain, Transparent, Translucent, Unshackled, Unmistaken
COIN	(See List of Coins) Make, Mint, Fake, Metal, Wedge, Stamp, Money, Quoin, Forge, Angle, Corner, Invent
COG	Cod, Rob, Fob, Boat, Catch, Cheat, Tooth, Cogie, Seduce, Coggie, Thrust, Entice, Cajole, Corrupt, Wheedle, Assault, Deceive
CLOSE	By, At, In, On, Mean, Near, Dear, Shut, Draw, Stop, Seel, Seal, Lane, Line, Fill, Damp, Worn, Alley, Solid, Dense, Unite, Place, Exact, Entry, Foggy, Pause, Finish, Narrow, Hidden, Stingy, Secret, Nearly, Nearby, Intent, Densely, Compact, Private, Tightly, Cadence, Grapple, Confine, Enclose, Consent, Precise, Guarded, Concise, Intimate, Familiar, Secretly, Encounter, Confined, Junction, Stagnant, Confined, Accurate, Reserved, Relaxing, Conclude, Complete, Compressed, Oppressive, Restricted
COCK	Hay, Tap, Set, Put, Man, Bird, Nose, Fowl, Vane, Fane, Walk, Pile, Heap, Chap, Male, Lock, Draw, Boat, Nock, Style, Place, Erect, Strut, Notch, Natch, Boast, Dignity, Bluster, Swagger, Weathercock, Weathervane
COLOUR	Bay, Dye, Eye, Red, Set, Hue, Jet, Dun, Tan, Pale, Mood, Paly, Blue, Blee, Kind, Pink, Rose, Dark, Tone, Ashy, Dull, Grey, Gray, Roan, Drab, Fair, Tint, Fawn, Puce, Ruby, Gold, Blae, Black, White, Tinge, Stain, Flush, Blush, Shade, Green, Brown, Paint, Grain, Sepia, Ashen, Sable, Hazel, Olive, Rouge, Flame, Pearly, Cherry, Russet, Orange, Yellow, Murrey, Bright, Mellow, Sallow, Florid, Purple, Violet, Indigo, Nigger, Sensation, Colouring, Temper, Timbre, Excuse, Quality, Pretext, Vividness, Character, Animation
COMFORT	Ease, Eath, Rest, Easy, Calm, Lull, Balm, Glee, Cheer, Peace, Quiet, Abate, Allay, Soften, Please, Smooth, Repose, Pacify, Soothe, Revive, Relief, Console, Condole, Compose, Support, Encourage, Enjoyment
CONDUCT	Lead, Head, Bear, Tend, Show, Shew, Guide, Teach, Coach, Carry, Escort, Convey, Direct, Convoy, Govern, Manage, Manege, Menage, Comport, Command, Control, Intrust, Guidance, Transmit, Behaviour, Direction, Treatment
COMPASS	Plot, Walk, Pass, Range, Fence, Limit, Space, Reach, Equip, Girth, Fulfil, Degree, Circle, Argue, Obtain, Needle, Invest, Circuit, Enclose, Inclose, Stretch, Besiege, Confine, Comprehend, Instrument, Accomplish
CONFIRM	Fix, Set, Fit, Agree, Found, Prove, Admit, Ratify, Assure, Verify, Certify, Testify, Testimony, Establish
CONSENT	Leave, Lease, Allow, Allot, Agree, Yield, Accord, Comply, Advice, Concord, Concert, Harmony, Compliance, Permission
CORK	Stop, Bark, Rine, Rind, Peel, Stopper, Stopple
CORRUPT	Rot, Low, Harm, Hurt, Foul, Soil, Base, Sell, Bribe, False, Defile, Putrid, Debase, Impure, Rotted, Rotten, Spoiled, Tainted, Unsound

COUNSEL Word, Warn, Ware, Plan, Form, Design, Advice, Advise, Barrister, Advocate, Opinion, Precept

CROCK Pot, Jar, Mug, Cup, Jug, Ewe, Smut, Soot, Fool, Coom, Dirt, Horse, Dirty, Shard, Person, Vessel, Blacken, Invalid, Pitcher

CRY Baa, Bay, Weep, Peep, Bawl, Yowl, Yawl, Gowl, Wail, Yell, Yelp, Pack, Call, Howl, Sound, Utter, Shout, Spout, Notice, Rumour, Lament, Squall, Prayer, Phrase, Declare, Exclaim, Proclaim, Announce

CUT Hew, Run, Gut, Rub, Mow, Saw, Clip, Trim, Chip, Chop, Hurt, Reap, Harm, Pass, Rift, Blow, Buff, Biff, Gash, Lash, Rash, Carve, Break, Piece, Wound, Allot, Knife, Sever, Shape, Cleft, Canal, Divide, Cleave, Detach, Gashed, Groove, Stroke, Trench, Scythe, Shorten, Intrude, Opening, Intersect, Penetrate, Mutilate, Separate, Channel

DARK Dim, Dun, Sad, Dirk, Deep, Drab, Grey, Gray, Black, Blind, Dusky, Dirty, Murky, Shady, Shaky, Opaque, Gloomy, Sombre, Hidden, Sullen, Shaded, Wicked, Secret, Obscure, Swarthy, Unknown, Uncertain, Obscurity, Concealed

DASH Mar, Mix, Rush, Clam, Ruin, Mark, Blow, Bash, Lash, Smite, Abash, Erase, Wreck, Break, Throw, Spoil, Onset, Daunt, Check, Strike, Action, Destroy, Unbuild, Sprinkle, Confound, Overturn, Collision, Frustrate

DEAD Cold, Dull, Deaf, Sure, Deep, Still, Quiet, Utter, Blank, Block, Vapid, Beaten, Deaden, Unreal, Inactive, Insipid, Useless, Benumbed, Deceased, Obsolete

DECLINE Turn, Bend, Drop, Fall, Fail, Sink, Shun, Decay, Stoop, Evade, Evite, Elude, Droop, Refuse, Reject, Disown, Deviate, Depress, Disease

DELAY Stop, Stay, Stow, Defer, Deter, Tarry, Dally, Pause, Waste, Dilute, Detain, Retard, Hinder, Hamper, Linger, Temper, Postpone, Stoppage, Stopping

DESERT Run, Cut, Rat, Tract, Waste, Leave, Merit, Claim, Close, Forsake, Abandon, Barren, Reward

DOG Pup, Pug, Cur, Cub, Pom, Rug, Bar, Hook, Cock, Pawl, Paul, Pone, Male, Worry, Harry, Tease, Harass, Person, Device, Fellow, Follow, Attend

DOLE Woe, Wae, Sad, Bad, Bit, Dose, Poin, Alms, Deal, Shore, Blow, Grief, Labour, Sorrow, Throes, Gloomy, Dismal, Torment, Portion

DRAG Rug, Tug, Lug, Move, Draw, Push, Pull, Tear, Coax, Hang, Hook, Haul, Harl, Fish, Sled, Cart, Coach, Trail, Trawl, Train, Scent, Force, Break, Pluck, Propel, Harrow, Entice, Search, Sledge, Difficulty, Impediment

DRESS (*See* Articles of Dress, etc.) Don, Cut, Dub, Put, Rub, Rig, Fig, Fit, Set, Hib, Trim, Deck, Cook, Comb, Dick, Garb, Style, Curry, Order, Adorn, Apply, Equip, Prune, Adapt, Array, Clothe, Attire, Cleanse, Prepare, Clothes, Provide, Apparel, Appoint, Arrange, Furnish, Garments, Decorate

DROP Lie, Die, Drip, Spot, Spit, Spat, Rain, Fall, Trap, Sink, Pour, Write, Leave, Lower, Utter, Device, Insert, Extent, Liquid, Liquor, Dismiss, Speckle, Globule, Descent, Quantity, Particle, Collapse

DRIVE Aim, Dig, Rush, Push, Send, Tend, Road, Urge, Edge, Ride, Hunt, Force, Hurry, Argue, Knock, Guide, Press, Impel, Chase, Course, Direct, Convey, Propel, Compel, Strike, Carriage, Argument, Distress, Overwork, Constrain, Prosecute

DULL Sad, Dim, Bad, Tan, Dun, Wan, Damp, Slow, Lash, Late, Blunt, Heavy, Dense, Sully, Obtuse, Obtund, Gloomy, Cloudy, Sullen, Tedious, Stupefy, Drowsy, Sleepy, Stupid, Dreary, Overcast, Sluggish, Tarnished, Wearisome, Depressing, Insensible

DRUM Drub, Oust, Beat, Hill, Play, Seek, Call, Ridge, Repel, Eject, Summon, Tomtom, Tamtam, Tumtum, Cylinder, Tympanum

EXPRESS Say, Put, Emit, Fast, Form, Press, Direct, Force, State, Clear, Haste, Train, Utter, Elicit, Extort, Reveal, Betoken, Exhibit, Resemble, Explicit, Definite

EYE Bud, See, Spy, Aim, Dye, Hole, Loop, Iris, Note, Ring, Look, Face, Care, View, Watch, Organ, Globe, Pupil, Sight, Tinge, Guard, Catch, Centre, Regard, Appear, Center, Notice, Observe, Subject, Eyeball

FAIR Just, Pure, Mere, Bare, Good, Open, Free, Clear, Clean, Frank, Civil, Plain, Light, Woman, Market, Beauty, Bright, Blonde, Candid, Honest, Melting, Legible, Comely, Lovely, Bazaar, Hopeful, Moderate, Gleaming, Plausible, Impartial, Beautiful, Collection, Prosperous

FALL Dip, Dib, Ebb, Cry, Die, End, Cut, Fell, Emit, Drop, Drip, Sink, Rush, Pass, Vade, Bout, Lapse, Light, Event, Issue, Yield, Death, Occur, Befall, Happen, Vanish, Outlet, Appear, Decline, Decease, Descend, Descent, Delapse, Relapse

FANCY Flam, Whim, Sham, Idea, Love, Image, Breed, Taste, Hobby, Figure, Object, Imagine, Portray, Caprice, Elegant, Faculty, Delusion, Illusion

FORCE Vim, Vis, Push, Rush, Gush, Draw, Fall, Army, Arms, Navy, Body, Power, Glory, Force, Cause, Stuff, Stress, Strive, Strike, Energy, Troops, Compel, Violate, Forbear, Validity, Violence, Strength, Coercion, Efficacy, Vehemence, Influence, Momentum, Overpower, Constrain, Animation, Stimulate

FUSS Ado, Ail, Speed, Haste, Hurry, Motion, Tumult, Labour, Bustle, Jostle, Flurry, Trouble, Agitate, Commotion, Agitation

FORM Norm, Plan, Mode, Rule, Make, Type, Kind, Cast, Last, Sort, Shape, Adapt, Model, Frame, State, Mould, Order, Class, Beauty, System, Adjust, Method, Settle, Ritual, Elegance, Practice, Ceremony, Contrive, Constrict, Symmetry, Procedure, Appearance, Arrangement, Disposition

GAME Nap, Loo, Pit, Put, Tag, Tig, Taw, Toy, Top, Brag, Grab, Golf, Goff, Gowf, Polo, Solo, Loto, Ludo, Ball, Bull, Pool, Faro, Mora, Snap, Skat, Lark, Race, Play, Sport, Lotto, Halma, Whist, Cards, Whisk, Poker, Bowls, Chess, Rummy, Rugby, Monte, Quoits, Shinny, Shindy, Shinty, Hockey, Hookey, Bridge, Soccer, Tennis, Stake, Jest, Trick, Dodge, Cricket, Plucky, Gamble, Lame, Crooked, Gambol, Frolic, Merriment, Diversion, Contest, Spirited

GO Pep, Vim, Vis, Fly, Ply, Pass, Walk, Tend, Wend, Mush, Rush, Turn, Move, Rove, Wind, Fare, Lead, Flow, Head, Haste, Start, Avail, Apply, Leave, Depart, Desert, Extend, Energy, Affair, Matter, Travel, Proceed, Advance

GOOD Fit, Pat, Apt, Boon, Gift, Well, Weal, Safe, Kind, Pure, Sure, Full, Real, High, Feal, Leal, Sane, Able, Brave, Whole, Moral, Pious, Godly, Right, Valid, Sound, Proper, Polite, Useful, Virtue, Welfare, Serious, Genuine, Skilful, Cheerful, Faithful, Suitable, Splendid, Virtuous, Pleasant, Righteous, Benevolent

HAND Side, Lead, Furl, Help, Hind, Limb, Agent, Power, Skill, Style, Index, Point, Guide, Handle, Finger, Servant, Control, Workman, Conduct, Handiwork, Authority

HEART Seat, Form, Mind, Core, Love, Soul, Saul, Zeal, Centre, Center, Spirit, Vigour, Ardour, Bravery, Courage

HELP Give, Keep, Heed, Serve, Avail, Assist, Remedy, Supply, Relief, Succour, Relieve, Provide, Support, Prevent, Servant, Further

HARD Mean, Tart, Sour, Firm, Near, Close, Miser, Beach, Cruel, Rough, Solid, Tough, Stiff, Tight, Severe, Stingy, Scanty, Coarse, Hoarse, Unjust, Unkind, Compact, Miserly, Difficult, Intricate

HIGH Fell, Loud, Good, Dear, Near, Sharp, Great, Grand, Acute, Aloft, Upper, Lofty, Chief, Proud, Noble, Remote, Shrill, Elevated, Arrogant, Excellent, Dignified

HOLD Set, Pit, Bind, Keep, Hole, Stop, Grip, Mark, Grasp, Clasp, Stand, Peace, Gripe, Esteem, Endure, Clutch, Adhere, Cavity, Derive, Defend, Support, Contain, Refrain, Possess, Believe, Maintain, Restrain

JACK Ball, Coat, Mail, Pike, Fish, Lift, Male, Flag, Tree, Screw, Knave, Fruit, Wedge, Sailor, Sailer, Device, Bottle, Fellow, Support, Pitcher

KNOT Pad, Tie, Bow, Bur, Nur, Nub, Join, Node, Gnar, Snar, Snag, Knag, Knur, Bird, Bond, Knot, Unite, Twist, Knurr, Joint, Perplex, Problem

LAY Lie, Set, Put, Sit, Bet, Bed, Song, Aria, Beat, Calm, Balm, Wager, Apply, Field, Allay, Place, Spread, People, Impose, Charge, Impone, Present, Conjoin, Produce, Deposit

LABOUR Work, Toil, Moil, Soil, Roll, Duty, Task, Role, Pains, Pitch, Exert, Strive, Effort

LASH Slow, Soft, Flog, Cord, Whip, Beat, Belt, Dash, Thong, Slack, Loose, Drive, Fasten, Secure, Strike, Stroke, Censure, Scourge, Assail

LET Cause, Allow, Grant, Lease, Delay, Permit, Suffer, Hinder, Impede, Retort

LIGHT Gay, Day, Sun, Ray, Down, Fair, Idle, Lamp, View, Airy, Rest, Fire, Easy, Clear, Dizzy, Quick, Sight, Giddy, Loose, Sandy, Wight, Active, Nimble, Beacon, Wimble, Alight, Candle, Kindle, Fickle, Bright, Window, Slight, Gentle, Lively, Settle, Aspect, Elegant, Trivial

LOB   Fish, Lout, Ball, Last, Hang, Impend, Depend, Fellow

LUG   Rod, Ear, Rug, Tug, Ton, Pull, Lobe, Draw, Haul, Harl, Twig, Mark, Drag, Trail, Trawl, Perch

LOOSE   Fag, Sag, Undo, Free, Lag, Slack, Vague, Relax, Slovenly, Careless, Unsettled, Uncertain, Discharge, Unfasten

MAKE   Form, Tend, Move, Mate, Male, Equal, Feign, Frame, Force, Reach, Create, Effect, Perform, Execute, Produce, Provide, Consort, Fashion, Prepare, Pretend, Construct, Establish, Contribute, Accomplish

MANNER   Sort, Kind, Mode, Habit, Style, Method, Custom, Address, Bearing, Character, Behaviour, Demeanour, Mannerism

MEAN   Base, Rank, Lean, Weak, Bear, Moan, Poor, Sordid, Design, Middle, Mesial, Median, Medial, Degree, Centre, Denote, Convey, Intend, Lament, Purpose, Signify

MORTAL   Fatal, Feral, Fated, Drunk, Being, Person, Deadly, Tedious, Extreme

MOULD   Dust, Rust, Musk, Mool, Make, Soil, Cast, Last, Form, Build, Shape, Earth, Grave, Cover, Knead, Fashion, Pattern, Fungoid, Produce, Fungus, Matrix, Ground

MOVE   Run, Cut, Bow, Bob, Rove, Walk, Skip, Skit, Step, Stir, Pace, Wake, Gait, Draw, Pull, Drag, Haul, Harl, Stir, Tread, Carry, Rouse, Roust, Cause, Touch, Shift, Slope, Elope, Alter, Impel, Tempo, Excite, Incite, Salute, Change, Affect, Neglect, Propose, Provoke, Proceed, Agitate, Prevail, Progress, Movement

NARROW   Way, Gap, Gat, Col, Pass, Near, Mean, Close, Small, Exact, Short, Stingy, Greedy, Strait, Strict, Confine, Reduce, Limited, Careful, Bigoted, Precise, Confined, Contract, Accurate

NEAT   Cow, Apt, Fib, Pat, Prim, Trim, Trig, Tidy, Deff, Oxen, Deft, Feat, Nice, Fine, Pure, Mere, Bare, Clean, Clear, Adept, Chaste, Spruce, Clever, Dainty, Adroit, Cattle, Simple, Single, Semple, Bovine, Subtle, Agreeable, Dexterous, Undiluted

NOTE   Re, Ti, Si, Mi, Fa, La, Sol, Soh, Doh, See, Eye, Spy, Air, Key, Jot, Mob, Sign, Heed, Mark, Tune, Tend, Tone, Bill, Fame, Name, Dame, Cave, Word, Token, Totem, Sound, Sight, Paper, Record, Repute, Report, Notice, Letter, Remark, Attend, Renown, Account, Comment, Quality, Information, Observation

NUMBER   One, Two, Six, Sum, Any, Add, Tot, Odd, Five, Nine, None, Even, Host, More, Herd, Pack, Unit, Many, Zero, Some, Seven, Eight, Forty, Fifty, Sixty, Issue, Verse, Metre, Count, Eleven, Twelve, Twenty, Thirty, Ninety, Reckon, Amount, Charge, Measure, Compute, Collect, Multiply, Multiple

PEER   See, Eye, Spy, Peep, Peek, Perk, Lord, Earl, Jarl, Duke, Look, Seem, View, Noble, Baron, Equal, Appear, Glance

PART   Bit, Ort, Fig, Lot, Cut, Tear, Rend, Rift, Side, Fate, Sift, Sort, Bolt, Role, Quit, Piece, Shave, Shove, Party, Sever, Break, Crock, Number, Resign, Retire, Member, Melody, Sunder, Divide, Divisor, Portion, Concern, Fortune, Section, Quantity, Fragment, Division, Interest, Separate

PASS   Go, Do, Col, Die, Run, Cut, Way, Move, Mush, Emit, Move, Omit, Slip, Skip, Scum, Road, Line, Lane, Pace, Walk, Flow, Fall, Fail, Stay, Send, Utter, Spend, Occur, Outdo, Outgo, Throw, State, Excel, Enact, Cause, Elapse, Charge, Ticket, Ratify, Exceed, Elapse, Thrust, Vanish, Strain, Defile, Narrow, Surpass, Undergo, Happen, Approve, Sanction, Transfer, Pronounce, Disappear, Circulate

PICK   Dig, Dip, Eat, Cull, Pull, Call, Peck, Tool, Open, Pink, Break, Stead, Steal, Clean, Prick, Pluck, Point, Choose, Choice, Pierce, Pilfer, Select, Gather, Garner, Strike, Nibble, Collect, Acquire, Implement, Selection

PLACE   Put, Set, Fix, Lay, But, Ben, Den, Pen, Way, Sit, Gite, Site, City, Town, Dive, Hive, Rank, Room, Spot, Dwell, Topic, Office, Garret, Bring, State, Settle, Invert, Castle, Locate, Locale, Dignity, Mansion, Village, Arrange, Portion, Station, Position, Priority, Vicinity, Vicinage, Condition, Locality, District, Situation, Residence

PIPE   Call, Play, Cask, Peep, Note, Tube, Roll, Chirp, Chirr, Chirk, Chirm, Sound, Utter, Noise, Clock, Cluck, Clack

PLAIN   Bare, Mere, Flat, Even, Open, Pure, Ugly, Easy, Free, Bland, Llano, Level, Clear, Clean, Homely, Honest, Modest, Lovely, Simple, Evident, Sincere, Artless, Clearly, Cleanly, Apparent, Manifest

POINT — Aim, Nib, Neb, Nub, End, Dot, Tip, Top, Pin, Show, Shew, Mark, Tick, Unit, Turn, Part, Spot, Stop, Cape, Naze, Ness, Gest, Gist, Jist, Lace, Fill, Type, Prick, Stage, Space, Thing, Place, Order, Verge, Sting, Guide, Detail, Moment, Direct, Degree, Switch, Design, Meaning, Quality, Purpose, Sharpen, Subject, Intimate, Indicate, Punctuation, Promontory

POT — (*See* List of Vessels) Lot, Dot, Set, Pop, Sow, Money, Drain, Float, Drink, Prize, Shoot, Snipe, Plant

POUND — Pin, Pen, Net, Ton, Tun, Bit, Hit, Fix, Set, Shut, Unit, Coin, Note, Beat, Bray, Money, Limit, Thump, Knock, Break, Wreck, Weight, Bruise, Buffet, Strike, Measure, Confine

PRESS — Dun, Run, Lay, Pay, Hug, Push, Urge, Bear, Rush, Hurry, Worry, Harry, Crush, Frush, Force, Clasp, Clamp, Swarm, Shape, Crawl, Prink, Weigh, Exert, Carry, Stress, Smooth, Closet, Throng, Compel, Rabble, Machine, Squeeze, Impress, Embrace, Compress, Condense, Distress

PUFF — Pad, Wad, Air, Bid, Fuff, Huff, Blow, Fill, Gust, Move, Wind, Boom, Ball, Whiff, Blast, Boast, Drive, Swell, Hurry, Pastry, Elate, Praise, Bustle, Breath, Breeze, Breathe, Inflate

PURL — Ale, Hem, Run, Flow, Nose, Loop, Beer, Rush, Curl, Eddy, Knit, Purr, Swirl, Twirl, Twist, Sweep, Ripple, Murmur, Bubble, Gurgle

PUSH — Bunt, Butt, Move, Urge, Sack, Pack, Rush, Stab, Drive, Shove, Impel, Press, Burst, Force, Strive, Attack, Hasten, Crisis, Thrust, Effort, Excite, Incite, Energy, Compel

PUT — Pit, Set, Lay, Sap, Say, Oaf, Try, Bed, Add, Tot, Push, Putt, Game, Cast, Turn, Hole, Clown, Throw, Drive, Yokel, Bring, Tempt, State, Trial, Utter, Place, Apply, Cause, Offer, Shoot, Steer, Effort, Impose, Incite, Entice, Oblige, Action, Thrust, Attempt, Deposit, Propose, Suggest, Assault, Express, Present, Subject

QUIET — Rest, Ease, Cosy, Easy, Eath, Calm, Balm, Lull, Mild, Dull, Cool, Still, Peace, Sleep, Abate, Allay, Repose, Smooth, Placid, Gentle, Pacify, Hushed, Silent, Appease, Retired, Comfort, Peaceful, Tranquil

RACE — Run, Cut, Fly, Root, Line, Clan, Raze, Rase, Herd, Pace, Rush, Stock, Tribe, Breed, Trial, Speed, Series, Family, Nation, Ginger, Career, Strain, Course, Motion, Vigour, Canter, Variety, Flavour, Descent, Current, Contend, Lineage, Channel, Contest

RACK — Fly, Bar, Net, Hack, Jack, Ruin, Tear, Draw, Wine, Pain, Neck, Cony, Veal, Pace, Gait, Grate, Frame, Shake, Drift, Sheep, Spine, Drive, Doubt, Worry, Tease, Exert, Wrest, Clouds, Mutton, Liquor, Engine, Strain, Extend, Injure, Vapour, Device, Torture, Stretch, Grating, Extension, Framework

RAISE — Lift, Puff, Rise, Call, Riot, Stir, Rear, Bear, Levy, Build, Erect, Extol, Hoise, Hoist, Yield, Breed, Rouse, Roust, Roist, Swell, Praise, Remove, Recant, Expand, Muster, Excite, Incite, Create, Summon, Gather, Collect, Produce, Inflame, Elevate, Exhibit, Forward, Promote, Advance

ROLL — Rock, Reel, List, Leet, Sway, Poll, Turn, Wrap, Bind, Peal, Move, Beat, Ruff, Gait, Mass, Loaf, Drive, Sound, Bread, Press, Paper, Inwrap, Volume Record, Roller, Register, Cylinder, Document, Revolve, Swagger, Flatten

ROUND — Orb, Arc, Big, Beat, Walk, Turn, Bold, Oval, Arch, Move, Full, Open, Stcp, Song, Large, Brisk, Frank, Smart, Quick, Plain, Globe, Orbit, Whole, Large, Plump, Ample, Scope, Volley, Smooth, Candid, Circle, Cirque, Sphere, Virole, Rundle, Flowing, Routine, Passage, Positive, Cylinder, Rotation, Encircle, Engirdle, Circular

ROW — Oar, Tar, War Jar, Mag, Din, Rag, Rig, Hag, Rank, Line, Rate, Rage, Roll, File, Brawl, Scold, Abuse, Noise, Tumult, Series, Uproar, Injure, Propel, Arrange, Upbraid, Quarrel

RUN — Dun, Fly, Ply, Sew, Bye, Fall, Melt, Bolt, Fuse, Fuze, Pour, Move, Push, Rush, Slip, Pass, Flee, Flow, Race, Turn, Dart, Sail, Skip, Cast, Trip, Hurry, Haste, Slide, Glide, Shoot, Reach, Force, Drive, Creep, Incur, Score, Chose, Tense, Evade, Brook, Range, Press, Voyage, Hasten, Manage, Travel, Melted, Extend, Pursue, Pierce, Thrust, Become, Course, Elapse, Spread, Period, Stream, Ground, Contend, Venture, Average, Clamour, Execute, Compete, Complete, Continue

SAFE — Sure, Room, Sane, Sage, Hale, Well, Wise, Chest, Place, Sound, Clever, Certain, Whole, Secure, Trusty, Strong, Entire, Perfect, Healthy, Prudent, Cautious

SAVAGE	Wild, Rude, Nude, Keen, Bare, Naked, Being, Cruel, Beast, Blunt, Brutal, Fierce, Person, Untamed, Furious, Inhuman, Barbarian, Primitive
SEND	Lend, Tend, Pack, Sack, Push, Hurl, Cast, Emit, Throw, Drive, Grant, Leave, Impel, Dismiss, Forward, Diffuse, Compel, Excite, Bestow, Propel, Transmit, Dispatch
SET	Fix, Fit, Let, Sit, Put, Sow, Flow, Stud, Join, Firm, Sink, Pass, Pose, Place, Pitch, Plant, Build, Adapt, Rigid, Point, Fixed, Twist, Mount, Adorn, Frame, Shape, Stick, State, Become, Number, Locate, Spread, Formal, Attach, Settle, Fasten, Normal, Furnish, Dispose, Replace, Appoint, Concrete, Prepare, Decline, Arrange, Regular, Congeal, Sharpen, Descent, Compose, Bearing, Carriage, Regulate, Obstruct, Stationary, Motionless
SORT	Fit, Put, Sift, Bolt, Kind, Race, Rank, Suit, Pick, Part, Cull, Style, Class, Adapt, Order, Degree, Manner, Reduce, Unwell, Select, Divide, Punish, Adjust, Fashion, Species, Disunite, Separate
STOP	Stem, Stay, Rest, Sist, Mark, Cease, Pause, Close, Check, Stuff, Delay, Tarry, Dally, Arrest, Stanch, Impede, Hinder, Hamper, Obstruct, Restrain, Obstacle, Punctuate, Cessation
STRIKE	Hit, Tap, Rap, Run, Pat, Slap, Find, Swat, Slay, Slat, Dash, Hook, Coin, Blow, Bump, Biff, Buff, Cuff, Pass, Dart, Fade, Stroke, Stripe, Stamp, Touch, Lower, Smite, Sound, Erase, Punish, Pierce, Thrust, Affect, Ratify, Afflict, Impress, Collide
TURN	Move, Veer, Wear, Fold, Form, Send, Spin, Walk, Bend, Tire, Slue, Sour, Swirl, Whirl, Avert, Twirl, Adapt, Issue, Hinge, Shape, Rebel, Blunt, Direct, Round, Apply, Alter, Repent, Curdle, Depend, Result, Return, Tumble, Manner, Change, Crisis, Revolve, Reverse, Deviate, Convert, Winding, Tendency, Occasion, Translate, Transform, Transmute
VIEW	See, Eye, Look, Show, Range, Scene, Survey, Vision, Sketch, Aspect, Inspect, Examine, Opinion, Picture
WASTE	Loss, Lose, Vain, Void, Wear, Tear, Empty, Spoil, Spend, Decay, Impair, Desert, Refuse, Injure, Injury, Unused, Region, Damage, Exhaust, Useless, Destroy, Dwindle, Consume, Decline, Country, Mischief, Squander, Desolate, Diminish

Made and Printed in Great Britain by
The Greycaine Book Manufacturing Company Limited, Watford